THE
ISLE OF DOGS

MEMORY AND CHANGE
IN THE 20TH CENTURY

A BRIEF HISTORY
VOLUME II

AN ISLAND HISTORY TRUST
PUBLICATION
BY EVE HOSTETTLER

Eve Hostettler is the curator of the Island History Trust
She has worked with the project since 1980

Canary Wharf, April 2002

Foreword

This book has been written with the help and support of hundreds of individual Islanders who have contributed photographs, written and tape-recorded memories, and documents, to the Island History Trust Collection since it was founded in 1980. I hope the book will serve a double purpose: firstly, to bring back to life, for those who remember it or have heard it spoken of, something of the "old" Island of industry and the port; secondly, for those who are new to the Island, I hope it will bring them greater understanding of the place they might now call home, of how it used to be and of how it came to be as it was at the beginning of the twenty-first century.

Much has been omitted, for reasons of space, and this is particularly true of the final chapter, which is about the last two decades of the twentieth century. This extraordinary period in the Island's history deserves a fuller account and this must wait for memories and other sources to be collected and viewed from the standpoint of a later age.

Thanks are due to all the volunteers and supporters who help Island History, and particularly to the Trustees of the Isle of Dogs Community Foundation, who provide Island History with some of its funds; to the London Borough of Tower Hamlets, who also help with funds, and who maintain the invaluable Local Studies Archive in Bancroft Road Library; to Gill Riordan, for her meticulous work on the index; and to Derek Chambers, for his design work.

Past and present Trustees of Island History are Mrs Bessie Boylett, Mrs Rose Day, Mr Ted Johns, Mrs Barbara Liddell, Miss Doris McCartney, Mr John Penn, Mrs Ada Price, Mr Bill Price and Mr George Pye. It is thanks to them that the Trust exists and that this brief history of the Isle of Dogs has been published. (*The Isle of Dogs, A Brief History, Volume I, 1066-1918*, appeared in 2000.) Any errors and ommissions are, however, the responsibility of the author.

Eve Hostettler   February 2002

Barges in West India Docks, 1983.

Contents

The Inter-War Years

1. The Island Environment

The Isle of Dogs was described in 1926 as "...in many ways a backwater...unique...beyond the main stream ...the life of the people is dull and drab beyond description; there is nothing for the people between the Church and Settlement activities and the Public House..." (*St. Mildred's Annual Report*).

Many outsiders commented on the Island's isolation. The river hindered contact with the south bank, "the other side" as it was called, although Greenwich foot tunnel was packed night and morning with people who worked on the Island. The narrow access roads onto the Island from the rest of the East End wound along between the high dark walls of the docks. Those who couldn't afford the fares for the little motor buses which trundled round had to "walk the walls". Pedestrians and riders all suffered from the "bridgers", when the road bridges crossing the entrance locks were raised to allow vessels in and out of the docks, a procedure which could last for half an hour or more. These factors all contributed to the Islanders' clannishness and a wary attitude towards "strangers".

By the 1920s the Island had lost most of its original rural charm. With its tall factory chimneys, railway lines and cobbled streets of terraced houses, encircled by the river and pervaded by the sights and sounds of the busy port, it was now part of a great trading city. The smoke from the chimneys blackened the atmosphere, accumulated in a layer of oily grime on the pavements and darkened the exterior of the buildings. If there was no cold breeze blowing in from the river, then as often as not one of London's damp and dirty fogs lay over everything. Except where newly-scrubbed doorsteps glimmered along the side streets in the early morning, and on Mondays, rows of washing, painfully whitened, fluttered on lines in backyards and gardens, the Island looked grimy and to the outsider, life there seemed rather gloomy and depressing. But the apparent bleak uniformity of run-down nineteenth-century housing and factories, with a common life-style centred round home, school, workplace and pub, was only part of the picture. Life was more varied and more rewarding than it looked.

There were many divisions within the Island. There were the two townships of Millwall and Cubitt Town, the former older and rather more cramped and dilapidated than the latter. The narrow width of Westferry Road, lined with early nineteenth-century cottages contrasted with the broader Manchester Road, with its more elegant mid-Victorian houses where short flights of steps lead up to a front door, and iron railings protected a basement area. Within each township there were further sub-divisions.

A "bridger" at the Millwall Dock entrance in Westferry Road

The bridge over the lock entrance to the Millwall Docks marked a distinction between north and south Millwall. In north Millwall bay-windowed houses in Strafford Street and Mellish Street could be distinguished as slightly more "posh" than the older, plainer terraces of the main road. In south Millwall the area from *The Kingsbridge* to *The Vulcan* pub was distinct from the Cahir Street/Hesperus Crescent area, whilst Chapel House Estate, although linked by a pedestrian bridge to Hesperus Crescent, was almost self-contained. Cubitt Town was divided into small neighbourhoods, varying in poverty and reputation. Glen Terrace, up by the bridge, verged on middle-class, being home to owners of small companies and to genteel women who gave piano lessons. Stewart Street, a stone's throw away, had a different aspect.

By the 1920s the Island population could be described as largely working-class, but there were many different trades and occupations within this. Some streets were associated with a particular trade. Launch Street was described by John Savage as "a veritable bastion of the Engineering and Allied trades." John's father Ted worked at Fraser's boiler shop in Wharf Road, his mother's father was a boilermaker, his brother Ted and John himself were boilermakers. Next door to them lived Jack Anderson, foreman at the London Graving Dock and near neighbours included Bill Hunt, foreman at East Ferry Road Engineering Works; Joe Hunt, foreman at the Aberdeen Steamship Company; Andrew Riley and Ernie Bowater, both sea-going boiler-makers, and Harold Phelvin, a sea-going carpenter and later foreman joiner at the London Graving Dock

Small neighbourhoods like this had their roots in the Island's nineteenth-century development. They maintained their identity in the inter-war years because young married couples often lived close to their parents, and children and adults followed the same routes every day – to visit grandparents, to get to school, to work, to the corner pub, to the local shops. School-leavers often went to work in the same place as their parents, aunts or uncles, and frequently courted and married within the locality.

In this way, individuals became very familiar with their own neighbourhood. Everyone's business was known and discussed, everyone's face was familiar, hence the common expression: "Everybody knew everybody else" – referring not to the whole 21,000 of the Island's population, but to the people routinely encountered every day, at school, at work and in the pub. This deep-rooted knowledge of environment and people contributed to the sense of security and well-being recalled by many of those who grew up there between the wars. For example:

"We had strict fathers and loving mothers and were taught to be kind and honest. We were able to walk safely in the streets at night, slept contentedly in our beds and loved our neighbours."

On the Mudchute allotments, 1922. Mr Brooker, stevedore, Charlie Clayden and Ernest Thomas, stevedore. The bench covers a well.

"Laughter abounded and...despite the poverty and austerity of that time, to a youngster there seemed much gaiety and happiness."

"...our lives on the Island were rich and colourful with not enough hours in the day to do all that we wanted..."

The Island still had some of the sights and sounds of the countryside. Alf French (born in 1917) remembered: "Most people around us seemed to have chickens because when one cock crowed in the morning a thousand crowed all around it, it was quite something, especially on a summer's morning when you had this early light. You heard this noise all round the Island, chickens and cocks cackling and crowing".

People kept rabbits and pigeons; there were still many horses. Corn chandler's shops flourished and hay and corn was carted about. Allotments created oases of beauty, behind *The Nelson* pub, on the Mudchute, along Stebondale Street, and at the end of Marsh Street, as James Mee recalled:

"Marsh Street used to be continued the other side of Cahir Street, there used to be four old cottages each side of this Marsh Street, and used to have a wooden fence at the end of this little street and you used to go through there and there used to be big allotments, it was beautiful, it was like being out in the country, at least for us kids, and course that was all taken away when they built those flats, you know." He also remembered the allotments on what is now Manchester Grove: "a profusion of colour, vegetables and flowers, the closest I got to the country for a long time".

Alf French described the typical allotment holder:

"From 2pm on a Saturday afternoon, after a morning's work and a hasty dinner (usually fish and chips, saveloy and pudding or sausage and mash) they would be wending their way along Farm Road (ie East Ferry Road) to the Mudchute. Trousers tied with string to keep the bottoms clear of wet grass or mud, sack and spade over the shoulder, and Woodbine drooping from the mouth, they would climb to their plot in the allotment area at the top of the Mudchute.

The first requirement was to look round and see what the neighbour was doing – how did he manage to ward off the carrot-fly? How does he get such a

Tony Atkinson, of Chapel House Street, with his friends in Westferry Road, during the late 1930s. Maconochie's Pan Yan Pickle factory in the background on the left.

good display of dahlias? A mental note was made to ask him next time he was encountered in the local, and the allotment holder then got down to weeding. The Mudchute seemed to produce an infinity of dandelions, colts-foot and milk-thistle seeds. Then it was time for the brassicas. The Island produced better cabbages than you could ever see in Chrisp Street or Salmon Lane and absolutely superb rhubarb.

The highlight of the year was the Harvest Festival. The churches borrowed barrows and these were piled high with cabbages, parsnips, marrrows and flowers. As children, the meaning of the Harvest Festival sermon was completely lost on us, our attention being riveted on the caterpillars climbing up the church walls – we wondered which would reach the roof first!

After the afternoon's work the allotment holder, boots caked in mud, sack filled with vegetables for Sunday and after, usually some for the mother-in-law and the neighbours as well, and a bit of groundsel for the canary or colts-foot for the rabbits, would wend

his way home with a possible call at the local for much-needed refreshment and an opportunity to expound to a captive audience the correct methods for producing prize beans or hearty lettuces."

The Mudchute was owned by the Port of London Authority. The entrances were guarded by the dock police, which made it all the more of an enticing adventure playground for children. They crept in through holes in the fence to play in the wild areas and catch tadpoles and newts in the land drain (the Newtie).

"They've always called it the Mudchute and they still call it the Mudchute. And there used to be a stream round the bottom of it. And the children there used to go and catch the tadpoles. They'd sit there for hours catching these tadpoles."

In the 1930s, according to Mr A. Learmouth, there were children's allotments in Stebondale Street, alongside the small Wesleyan Chapel, set up by the London Children's Garden Fund. He spent many happy hours there.

Another favourite childhood adventure was the long walk to Greenwich Park or Blackheath with jam sandwiches and a bottle of water, often taking younger children along in a pram.

There were hundreds of children on the Island and when not at school they were to be seen playing outside in all but the worst of weather. Football and cricket were popular in their seasons, and there were many street games, some of the best remembered being *Tibby Cat, Tin Can Copper* and *High Jimmy Knacker*:

"Tin can copper – what they did was to put a few tin cans on top of each other and they used to be about 10 yards away either end and then what you used to have to do was throw a ball, a tennis ball and you had to knock the tin cans down, and then once you knocked the tin cans down you all run away and hide. And then the opposing team had to find out where you all are and catch you.

And Tibby Cat used to be another one. What we used to do was get a bit of wood, sharpen both ends, rest it on the edge of the kerb and then you used to hit it with another stick and it used to fly up in the air, and as it flew up in the air you have to hit it with a stick as far as you can. and then when you get to the Tibby Cat again, you count the steps back to where you originally hit it and if you can get so many steps, well, you are the winner.

Then another one was High Jimmy Knacker. There used to be teams, about half a dozen in each, and then the six boys used to stand up against the

George Henry Wright, of 16 Strafford Street. George was engaged to Doris Coker and this picture was taken in the back yard of her home at 131 Westferry Road. They were married in St. Luke's Church on Boxing Day, 1926. Notice the chickens in the coop behind George.

wall, holding each other's shoulders, in a line, bent over. What the other team used to do, they used to run and jump onto the other people's shoulders or backs as far as they could go. They have to get all on, and then once they are all on, they say, High Jimmy Knacker, one two three, one two three, one two three, High Jimmy Knacker, one two three, all the over, all the over. And if they stay up, when they do that, they have won. But mostly, more often than not, they all fell off. That used to be a strenuous one, that did. Oh dear!"

Peggy Durham remembered the life of the streets:

"We always played under a lamp-post outside Mrs Black's house on the corner of Chapel House Street. Opposite was a little wooden shack which was

George Robinson kept his stall until the 1950s.

owned or rented by Mr Robinson who lived in East Ferry Road. We used to call him "Robbo". On his birthday he would buy as many ice-creams as his age and give them away to the local children.

There was always something going on in the streets, the water carts washing the roads, coalmen delivering coal – if he was in a good mood and his cart was fairly empty, he would let us have a ride – knife grinders. Pubs and shops had huge blocks of ice delivered – the delivery man had enormous tongs and he heaved the ice from the cart onto a piece of sacking. An old rag-and-bone man with a roundabout on his cart gave rides for empty jam jars. The highlight

was when the Lunar Boys came round with their barrel organ and gave us a show. The Lunar Boys were men dressed as women and used bad language. At night the toffee apple man came round, shouting out: 'ha'penny each or three a penny toffee apples'."

Dennis Dawson recalled that there were: "...cycles and seasons for doing things. At one time it might be the whip and top, at another it would be the hoop and stick. Then there would be the time for marbles when all children were in competition to see how many marbles they could accumulate." Another craze was the making of scooters, using bits of wood and two ball bearing races for wheels. "The noise of those steel wheels going over the pavements was quite satisfying and made all the work worthwhile." In the winter it was fun to make slides on the hard-packed snow.

Patrick Barry had fond memories of: "...the scrapyards, where as kids we could buy a front or back wheel, mudguards, chains, every part of a pushbike...all for a few coppers...the excitement of putting it together and riding it for the first time...older lads showed us how to hold the ball bearings with thick grease..."

The Island streets had dozens of small shops, general grocery stores, butchers, greengrocers, chandlers, and more specialised shops for pianos, drapery, bicycles and football boots. Most of these shops were open from early morning until well into the night, and when the shop was closed, it was customary to go to the side door. Looking back on her childhood Mrs Salmon calculated that there were 97 shops of different kinds in Westferry Road between Cuba Street and Glengall Road before the Second World War. According to George Thurgar, they included 16 which sold sweets (amongst other things) and: "... that's not counting the people who made toffee apples and trays of treacle toffee in their houses and sold them at the door or in the street." It was common for old people living alone to appear at their doorway and call the nearest child to go to the shop for them, fetching a bit of jam or a loaf of bread or whatever small item was needed. Here is one shopping routine recalled from 1918:

"...you are standing on the corner of Roserton Street and Manchester Road. The shop there is Saunders, a corn chandler. You go in there for a pint of dry peas, not soaked ones – Mum says you don't get so many. Next you cross the road to Edgar May's where you get five pounds of potatoes for tuppence and one penny worth of pot herbs, ask for most onions. Next door, at Price's General Stores, you join the Christmas Farthing Club, two shares for a ha'penny. Cross the Road to Obrarts the fish shop and get a tupenny-ha'penny haddock; next door to Alan's paper shop to get the children's newspaper, cross the road again here is Medlock's, the baker, Mum gets stale bread cheaply; go along to Ben Hucke's and get a ha'pennorth of Blackman's coconuts, they are small hard kernels which you soak.

Shop-keeping families: Walter James Williams, a clerk in the lead works; Griff Noall; Gladys Williams (nee Leeds) and her husband Walter; Fred Williams; Arthur Williams; in front, Elizabeth Williams (nee Gaskin); Louie, Griff's wife; Grandma Ellis, mother of "Grandma" Noall; Griff's mother; a widow, she kept a chandler's shop in Manchester Road. The little girl is Gwen Noall, later Payne

Get a liquorice stick for your brother, on the way back call at Gentry's for a fourpenny ox-tail and a lump of suet, cross the road again, past Womball's the chemist and Wiseman's, go next door to Tingay's the linen draper, the door bell will clatter and the parrot will keep calling "Shop"; after a time an old lady will appear and so you buy some ribbon for your hair. Next walk to the *Queen Hotel* to cross the road, but be careful, the buses come over the bridge hill at about 18 or 20 miles an hour; on the corner you go to Dolly Locke's, once again the door bell rings and once again the parrot: "Shop!". You buy sugar. Dolly gets some stiff blue paper, rolls it into a cone and then flaps the top down. You go round the corner to Number 14 Stewart Street and home."

There were more shops "round the other side" in Westferry Road:

"Aunt Polly was an old fashioned sweet shop in Westferry Road near the Harbinger Road School. She was a kindly old lady, always scrupulously clean and always dressed in a dark serge dress with lace collar and cuffs, with round her waist, a pure white frilled apron. The favourite sweet for kids was Milk Toffee, which Aunty made herself.

Another shop was a butcher's, the converted front room of a two-storey house. Albert and his assistant were open all hours, until nearly midnight on Saturdays. There was always lively conversation and saucy chatter with the women. Wally's oil shop stood next door. It was run by two brothers and a third brother who apparently lived a solitary life in a back room. As children we imagined he was a corpse they had hidden and so we were always wary of them! Further along the road stood the *Lord Nelson* public house opposite the Fire Station and the greengrocer

across the road. This was run by "Boston" Skeels, so called because of his haircut, the "Boston", a 'twenties style from America. He went round the streets with his horse and cart and could be heard streets away with his favourite call: "Apples-a-pound pears". Critchells the barber offered "short back and sides" for sixpence and "a good clean shave" for fourpence." Another fond memory is of the Italian family, Anastasio, who had a barber's shop and a greengrocery, and sold ice-cream and Sarsparilla, a popular drink."

There was still a great deal of horse-drawn traffic in the streets, and very few private cars, though motor lorries and buses were increasingly common. Bicycles were everywhere, there were telegraph boys, racing round on their bright red bikes, dressed in their uniforms complete with little pill-box hats, and errand boys:

"I got my first job at a place called Fenner and Alders, a paint factory, just opposite the then *Millwall Dock Tavern*, over the Millwall Dock Bridge on the left

Harry Burns of Millwall, photographed in Tooke Street with horse and cart belonging to William Stansell, cooper. William ran a carrying service from his home at 32 Tooke Street and took families down to Kent for the hopping.

The number 56 bus in Westferry Road near The Ship public house, with Chapel House Street behind the bus on the left hand side of the road.

hand side, as the road bears round....I was there for 18 months running messages here and there...they bought me a bike, with a big carrier on the front. And I used to cycle to the City with cans of paint, I went all round the West End of London...all round delivering cans of paint." (Bernard Bannister)

Patrick Barry remembered going to the cycle shop in Manchester Road with his first week's wages and buying a brand new Hercules, all shining paintwork and chrome, for sixpence or a shilling a week: "We would venture further and further afield, making our way out to Kidbrooke, a beautiful place unspoilt by urban sprawl. Grass, trees and a large lake. Quenching our thirst with a glass of home-made lemonade...it's all gone now."

The river and the docks, places of hard work for their fathers and older brothers, held an endless fascination for children when they were old enough to venture away from their own home and street:

"My early days were soaked by the sounds and smells of the sea and ships. When the tide was high the bridges were swung to allow the ships to come and go into the river and out to sea. This blocked the roads and we school children had to walk all round the docks from a gate one side, crossing the lock gates by a narrow wooden bridge which held the water high for the ships, to the other side and out again. We passed through the great warehouses full of coffee beans, cocoa beans, grain in great mountains, wine in barrels, nuts and tropical fruit. There were great stacks of timber from Russia and skins of fur and leather. There were also barrels of rum from Jamaica...We children were always late for school." (Alice Parmenter)

The coming and going of the sailing ships and steam ships stirred the imagination of young boys. In his autobiography, Bill Chapman recalled that the influence of his surroundings: "...started when I was about five or six years old. I was walking along Prestons Road with my Mum when I saw the bowsprit of a sail ship sticking over the wall and half way across the road. From that moment I was transported into a world from which I have never fully returned. To me there is nothing more beautiful than a fully rigged ship heeling with the wind, sadly a sight seen no more. The last two wind ships in Millwall Dock were the "Pamir" and "Passat".

I haven't seen the new dock area and I don't think I want to. I prefer to remember it as it was, with the hustle and bustle of port activity, the road transport queuing outside the gates waiting to be unloaded, the endless movement of shipping – Palm boats, Elder Dempster, Cunard, Furness, Blue Star, Maru boats. When I was a kid I could name almost every shipping company from their funnel markings. Then there were the two giant floating cranes, "Goliath" and "Leviathan", and of course the work horses of the river, the Sun tugs. It all added up to an education that could never be taught in a classroom."

Ship's bowsprit hanging over Westferry Road from the dry dock of Fletcher, Son & Fearnall, about 1920. The houses on the left were built in 1916. On the right, the dock walls. This is approximately the site of Westferry Circus, constructed in the 1990s.

Adventurous boys were drawn to the river:

"One or two other things that we used to get up to as young lads, where we lived in Stewart Street, was climbing over what we termed Stewart's Wall, that was a high wall that ran along the river, between the river and the street. There was always a bank of ground the other side of the wall. Well as young lads we used to climb over this wall and we'd play on the waste ground, or we may even be a bit more adventurous and go down to the quay, adjacent to the river, where we used to get down and go and swim in the Thames. And what we termed the senior boys, used to get up to some daring exploits, because when the tide came in, it came up to a fairly high level and there was one or two cranes along the quay, so I can remember quite vividly again, going up the crane with one of the senior boys, I would be on his back with my arms round his neck and he would dive into the Thames and we would then swim around and he would fetch me back, this didn't only happen to me it happened to other boys."

The river was a source of free goodies: "...carob syrup was used in desserts and sweets and things and these beans came over and they were often discharged in bulk into barges and therefore you could climb onto

12

the barge and you'd always find a place where the tarpaulin wasn't quite secure and of course you helped yourself to locust beans. Took them round all your friends and everybody was chewing locust beans and this kind of thing went on."(Alf French)

The river could be a threat to homes and lives. Mr Huish recalled that in Johnson Street, "...we would be awakened at night often to see the river, via the drawdock, passing down the street in cascades, and we would have to salvage furniture and other household goods from the basement as best we could. This usually happened at the time of the spring tides."

The worst of these floods was on a Saturday in January 1928. Joe Sullivan recalled: "...came over in 1928 and my sister Mary she was at home then and she said, Father, Father, the Thames is coming over. What did my father say? What do you want me to do, like King Canute, go and push it back? And it never reached our houses. It reached some of the houses that side of the road and the top end of Manilla Street, but it never reached our houses as we was No.52, we was about three parts down Manilla Street and I can always remember my father saying what do you want me to do, be like King Canute and go and push the water back?"

The *East London Observer* reported that following the flood warning: "...an army of men were employed for many hours in removing goods from wharves which were threatened with destruction. Many thousands of bales, barrels, crates and boxes containing all sorts of merchandise were removed to places of safety. Wharves, quays and docks have suffered great damage..."

The threat of flood only finally receded for Islanders with the opening of the Flood Barrier at Woolwich in 1982.

For the children, Island industry was their Disneyland. Running round, peeping through doorways, they saw gigantic structures, scary sights and colourful people. David Mulford, born in 1930, wrote of the ropeworks:

"A tremendously long shed, running alongside a ditch, housed the ropeworks and infinite lengths of string would be twisted eternally to make ropes for ocean liners. This twisting was done by a machine on rails and the sight of a "robot" approaching was awe-inspring to youngsters and quite often we would take fright and run like hell."

He went on: "Much of my childhood was spent in the grounds of C.& E.Morton and there were small pump-handled railway trucks to tamper with, the open water tank over the boiler house in which to sail home-made boats and the stack of metal steps leading to the small flour mill from which we launched home-made paper aeroplanes...sometimes the door of the large factory would be left open and we would

A "top cart" and ropemaker, laying rope in the ropewalk at Hawkins & Tipson's factory in East Ferry Road. The site was later commemorated with a planted walkway to Stebondale Street.

explore, to be confronted by enormous stores of glace cherries and candied peel."

And William Chapman remembered: "The Indian Lascar seamen, when they came ashore...all wore traditional long white robes… to me they were supermen. Small framed, skin and bone to look at, but the fantastic weights that they used to carry! Forty gallon drums full of clinker and ashes, slung on a pole carried from the stokehold, down the gangway, along the dock, to the ash heap..."

Peggy Gleeson recalled childish fears of the unknown: "Living near the dock gates we saw quite a lot of foreigners. I remember one day a crowd of black men in very bright clothing coming towards us. We were frightened and ran to Robbo's shop. He lifted us over his half-door (which was his counter) then shut the top and we all hid until they had gone by."

Mrs Betty Cocks (nee Hobby) lived at 81 Glengall Road, where her father was a watchmaker, jeweller and also sold gramophones and records: "He had contracts with many firms to keep the time clocks in order. I well remember going to some of the firms with him, early in the evening – Maconochie's, Morton's, Manganese Bronze works and others. I particularly liked the factories with the huge furnaces, the colours fascinated me but I must admit I was very scared."

The background to the life of the Island was a barrage of sounds, sounds which only faded away from Saturday afternoon to early Monday morning. Starting with the crowing of the cockerels and the blowing of factory whistles, the noise went on throughout the day and into the night. Ship's sirens hooted, especially in foggy weather; machinery hummed, rumbled and roared, drilled, hammered and sawed in the Island's many factories; horses and carts trundled noisily over the cobbled streets and motor vehicles added their engine sounds to the general hub-hub; street sellers called their wares, bicycles rattled along and delivery boys and telegraph boys in their smart uniforms sang or whistled as they rode busily about. Steam engines and the sound of railway wagons being shunted could be heard. The Millwall Extension Railway, which had been feeling the effects of competition from the new motor buses, closed in 1926 during the General Strike, and never re-opened, but there were many other lines carrying goods traffic, including the sidings which ran in and out of the docks, connecting the factories and warehouses to the Goods Depots of the Great Western Railway, and the London and North Eastern Railway, at Poplar Dock, East India Dock and Blackwall.

Added to all this was the sound of tramping feet as people walked to and from work or rushed out in

Railway bridge in Manchester Road. This bridge carried the Millwall Extension Railway over the road to the North Greenwich station on the river bank. The line closed in 1926 and the bridge and the urinal were demolished before the Second World War. A new bridge was built and the line reopened in 1987 to carry the Docklands Light Railway when it had a terminus at Island Gardens.

their dinner break for something to eat. Mavis Skeels remembered:

"At the top of Chapel House Street was Maconochie's jam and pickle factory; their slogan: "My – You're in a fine Pickle". Most of the workers were girls and women who wore clogs and white overalls and aprons with white turbans round their hair. A single railway line ran from the factory to the docks across the bottom end of our garden. The smell of pickles, vinegar and spices pervaded the air at all times. Noise and bustle were ever-present. At lunchtime the factory hands came tumbling out to buy their fish and chips at "Em's", short for Emily, who ran the shop. Some went to "The hole in the wall" a cafe across the street which literally was an opening in the wall with a couple of stalls and a tea bar. They sold sandwiches, hot dogs, doughnuts and filled rolls. A blast from the factory hooter sounded the end of the lunch break and the workers trooped back through the gates to continue their day's work until six or seven o'clock, having started at seven or seven-thirty in the morning."

The pungent smells from this particular factory joined a host of others in the Island atmosphere. Blocked drains and the polluted river stank in summer and the air was always smokey with the emissions of industrial and domestic chimneys, acrid with the smell of burning oils and processed chemicals and metals; added to this were the myriad aromas from the docks, of cattle feed, grains, spices, rum, sugar, rotting fruit, fresh fruit and a hundred other different cargoes.

The constant dust and dirt added to the burden of housework for the already over-worked Island women, whose daily life was a treadmill of cleaning, washing, cooking, ironing and mending as they laboured to feed and clothe their families.

Married women worked so hard they had little time for recreation. Some "kept themselves to themselves" apart from a weekly visit to church or chapel, but many women, when they had time to spare, sat outside, and on warm summer evenings Island streets were dotted with their figures in dark frocks and clean aprons, perched on low window sills or on chairs brought to the open door.

"There was no radio or television...and one of the ways people kept in touch was being part of what was going on outside. Anywhere in Poplar and of course the Isle of Dogs, particularly on a summer evening, you would see almost at every house, people sitting on chairs outside their front door, my mother used to do this and we looked across the road to the houses opposite and there was always someone sitting outside, if they weren't sitting on a chair they were sitting on their own window sill and every now and again you would talk to the people going by...and when you did come in, you said, "Oh I saw Mrs So-and-so going past and that Mr So-and-so I see has done this that or the other..." (Alf French).

Mrs Emily Hillier, nee Brown, and her daughter Betty, born in 1932, at the garden gate of No.3 Alpha Grove opposite the North Pole pub.

Late in the evening the Island's many pubs closed and their customers drifted homewards, and as they did so, the occasional argument broke out, sometimes ending in a quick exchange of blows. The noise woke the sleeping children who peered out of their windows into this adult world. On Fridays and Saturdays the singing which had begun in the pubs frequently continued with a party in someone's tiny front room.

George Hames listed some of the Island pubs in his autobiography: "There were over 30 pubs and some of them were the headquarters of various charitable and friendly societies such as the Foresters, Oddfellows, Masons and Buffaloes, and most of them had loan clubs. If any customer was on hard times through accident or illness, there was always a collection to help him, from his local. Some of the pubs were: *City Arms (later City Pride), North Pole, Blacksmith's Arms, Mechanics Arms, Anchor and Hope, Pin and Cotter, Pride of the Isle, The Islander, Tooke Arms, The Dockhouse, The Kingsbridge, Magnet and Dewdrop, The Vulcan, Glengall Arms, Great Eastern, Robert Burns,*

The Ship, Lord Nelson, Ferry House, Princess of Wales (known as "Mac's"), Newcastle Arms (later re-named Waterman's Arms), Pier Tavern, Builders' Arms, Dorset Arms, Cubitt Arms, The George, Manchester Arms, The London, The Queen".

Coffee shops and dining rooms were crowded at meal-times with hungry working men. George Hames listed some of them: "Bob Allen's at the dock gates in East Ferry Road; in Westferry Road there were Mrs Parker's Dining Rooms, the Anchor, the Old Barge, Tom King's Dining Rooms, and Kinchin's and Brunt's opposite each other at the bottom of Ferry Street. There were two large ones opposite *The George* and one by the dock gates near the Blue Bridge. There were others and this I will say of them all: good grub and good service."

Andrew Spring remembered that: "On the corner of Mellish Street, Len Ricks had a Coffee Shop. It would be full, the windows steamed up, cups and plates chinking, lots of babble, the smell of eggs, bacon, fried potatoes, tomatoes and fried bread would waft out, meeting our noses, just like the Bisto kids!"

During the inter-war years, the nature of the Island's environment altered very little. It remained a crowded industrial community, dominated by the sights and sounds of engineering works and factories, the river and the docks. The dock bridges and high walls still separated Islanders from the rest of the East End. By the end of the 1930s, people had not become noticeably richer, just a little bit better fed and smarter in appearance. There were less unemployed men, and more motor vehicles on the streets. Some of the worst of the old housing had been demolished and replaced by cottages and blocks of flats. Millwall Central School had been rebuilt in 1929, the Island Baths had been refurbished. Cubitt Town Recreation Ground (the New Park, later Millwall Park) had been created with its open air pool and in 1935 the new Cubitt Town School had been built in Saunders Ness Road.

In 1938 and 1939 preparations were being made for a war which was expected to bring aerial bombardment to London. The world the children had known was to become no more than a memory. In 1987 Peggy Reed (nee Freegrove) born 1928, wrote: "Some years ago I went on a tour of London which passed through the Isle of Dogs, but sadly did not recognize any of it. The old houses in Manchester Road with the basement kitchens and outside toilets, and tiny living rooms with black-leaded grates and cloth-covered mantlepieces with bobbles and fringes and gas mantle and brackets, had long since vanished into the past and now remain only in my mind's eye."

George Lawrence, of 95 Stebondale Street, "angle cropping" at Power Deane & Ransome's Engineering Works, Wharf Road, in the 1930s.

2. A Place to Work

In 1936 a publication from the Poplar Chamber of Commerce listed over 400 industrial firms in the E14 and E3 postal districts, from adhesive manufacturers to wool factors, from the exotic tortoiseshell makers in Brunswick Road to the heavy duty constructional engineers, Power Deane & Ransome's, in Wharf Road. This tremendous variety reflected London's importance as a centre of industry, and a great trading city. It also concealed the fact that by comparison with other parts of the capital in this period, East London was a black hole of poverty and unemployment.

The manufacture of new products such as electrical goods, cars and foodstuffs, was expanding in West London. Factories producing gramophones, canned food and other consumer goods, sprang up along the Great West Road in the 1920s and 1930s. Similar expansion was happening in North London and in Essex, but inner London did not attract the same new investment.

Many of the industries which had flourished around the port up to the beginning of the 20th century, now found themselves burdened with antiquated production methods, constricted space and inadequate transport systems. Some were able to relocate to larger premises. Duckham's Oil moved from Millwall to a site in west London in the 1920s, and later became a subsidiary of British Petroleum. Duckham's, and the new industries of West London, were producing for a growing home market, but there were older firms in Bow and Poplar which were dependent on traditional patterns of foreign trade, making them vulnerable to the ups and downs of international markets.

During the inter-war years, therefore, the story of the Island's economy was a mixed one. The port flourished, due to continuing overseas demand for British goods. Port-related industries such as packaging, rope-making and ship-repair, also survived well, as did those connected with expanding areas such as construction and motor transport or the manufacture of plastics. Others suffered from the decline in demand for their products, or from increasingly intense competition. Poor management and lack of investment also contributed to closure or to takeover by larger concerns.

In the 1920s Poplar's unemployment rate ranged from 10% to 20%, and remained at around 15% in the 1930s. These figures concealed a great deal of under-employment, due to the casual nature of cargo-handling and food processing. Nearly one quarter of Poplar's inhabitants were living in poverty in the late 1920s, and although the 1930s saw some improvement, it was easy for employers to exploit their workers. Low wages, overtime without pay and dangerous conditions, were commonplace. Trade unionism on the Island was weak by national standards, especially in the non-port-related industries and those which employed large numbers of unskilled and semi-skilled workers. Cole (1981) points to a tradition of strike-breaking and to a high turnover of women workers, as mitigating against strong union organisation.

"I left school in the October when I was 14 years old. My birthday was on Sunday and I started work the next day at C & E Morton's, until I was 16. Then I went to Woolworths at Lewisham for about three weeks and then started at Hawkins and Tipson until I was 20 and left to get married." (Island woman)

"Mum worked at Morton's factory making jam. She had to wear clogs because it was so sticky underfoot. She slipped one tragic day and put her arm into a pan of boiling syrup. She was in terrible

Women workers at Hooper's Cable and Telegraph Works in the Millwall Docks, 1930s. From left to right: Sarah Ferguson, Maggie West, Nell King, Grace Dyer, Kitty Fry, Dolly Harris and Hettie Stanley.

pain for weeks, her wedding ring had to be sawn off her finger and she carried the horrible scars to her grave. Later she went to work at Maconochies, making pickles." (Gladys Humphrey)

Another Island woman, born in 1922, after leaving school at 14 and trying various jobs, said: "I then went to work in MacDougall's factory in Millwall Docks, only a few minutes walk from home. The work consisted of sweeping up and getting bags and cartons for packing. You had to be 16 before you could go on the machines.

By the time I was 16 McDougalls had built a new factory and converted the old one into offices. This new factory made working conditions much easier. All employees were working seven hour shifts, which was strange at first, but gave us more free time.

When war was declared and men began to be called up, women replaced them in their jobs. I was asked if I would like to train in Laboratory work, which meant testing the wheat and flour. I enjoyed this work and remained in the Laboratory until our first child was born."

Port workers were united as much by family loyalties as by trade unionism. Bernard Bannister:

"We all went to St.Edmund's School. Crowds of us. the Wrights, the O'Briens, the McSweeneys, all went to St.Edmund's. My dear wife was in the second class. I didn't know her but she knew me...now I'm talking of the days before Montague Myers was even there, and our berth in those days was where now *The Daily Telegraph* is, and across the dock right the way down to McDougalls was all eight or nine or possibly 10 ships in the docks... they were great times, they were good times. We have got something to look back to. No one had nothing in those days, you know. My wife's family they was all stevedores, her dad was a stevedore, her brothers was all stevedores, so I more or less grew up with that crowd... But the characters in those days, I feel proud to have served with them... it wasn't a job, it was a way of life..."

The boys and girls in these dock-working families played together and went to school together, socialised together, worked in the same jobs, grew up and married into each other's families and settled down in the familiar streets. This pattern remained characteristic of port work until the docks closed, even when the communities were gradually dispersed by circumstances. George Pye senior said: "Nearly all stevedores knew one another as stevedores... I knew people over Canning Town, Custom House, thereabouts... One of our own, they used to say."

The culture of dock work was part of the life of the Island.

The endless variety of cargoes arriving from all over the world, the different shipping lines with their crews of many nations, the large and small companies associated with land- and river-based transport and storage, the vagaries of the weather and of the local, national and global markets, the dozens of wharves and the huge dock systems with their roads, railways, offices and warehouses – these were all part and parcel of everyday life for the workforce. There were thousands of men, working in all kinds of trades associated with cargo handling, transport and the movement of vessels, each trade having its own hierarchy and traditions. There were corn porters, deal porters, meat handlers, tally clerks, samplers and cask repairers, to name just a few. Once in the docks, the

Albert Conn, 1897-1974, whose account of his experiences on the front in World War One appear in Volume I of this Brief History. Albert went on to the permanent staff of the PLA and one of his jobs was crane-driving. He was also an artist and his work was exhibited in London.

Deal porters discharging timber in the Millwall Docks.

Tom Clark and Nell Vine on their wedding day in the 1920s. Tom was born at 51 Stebondale Street in 1906. He worked in Millwall Docks as a corn porter, and was also a union organiser.

young worker (who often acquired his place through family connections) learnt codes of conduct from his fellow workers, took part in decision-making either informally or through a trade union, and became part of a working team in which mutual trust and loyalty were paramount. In cargo-handling, co-operation was essential for the efficient completion of the work in hand and for safety . "A mistake could cost your life". Dock workers took care of each other in various ways, such as allocating light tasks to older or weaker members of a gang.

It was not an easy way of life. The work itself was physically exhausting – "sugar, if it was near the boilers, the sacks would be like gravestones, it was rock" – potentially dangerous and often very unpleasant: "If rats got amongst potatoes they would be putrid – the smell!" In a memory which highlights a child's awareness of adult troubles, Mavis Skeels described one of the jobs her father did:

"A cargo of brown sugar in one hundredweight and three hundredweight sacks had to be unloaded fast and the casual stevedores were taken on to speed up the process. These sacks had to be lifted and transported from the hold of the ship, humped onto the shoulders, then the back, and carried perilously across a gang plank to the quayside and dumped in the warehouse. This procedure, for hours on end, with the sacks sometimes splitting open and the contents trickling down the back, caused a lot of discomfort and soreness. But it was the best-paying job on the dockside for a casual, and my dad thanked Heaven for it."

The young dock worker also learnt that there were groups within groups, rivalry between gangs and between different unions, and fierce competition for jobs. There were two main unions within the docks and they were often at odds with each other. Members of the Transport and General Workers' Union, formed in 1922 out of 14 separate unions, were known as "the whites" (from the colour of their membership card). The unions which remained outside the TGWU formed themselves into The National Amalgamated Stevedores' and Dockers' Union, "the blues". Rivalry between the two was intense and could spill over into domestic life – marriage between "blue" and "white" families was discouraged.

Competition for work was most evident in the "call on". The Port of London Authority, formed in 1909 out of the old dock companies, had inherited the custom of supplementing its permanent workforce with men taken on for the day or half day, depending on the amount of work available. These workers were recruited at recognised points, one being opposite *The*

George pub in East Ferry Road, where Mrs Skinner recalled seeing men waiting in the 1930s: "...lining up each side...it would break your heart when you see them men...when they got a day's work, they had to pay all what they borrowed back...And I knew some of them had big families. There was more dinner times than dinners."

Stan Webb described the "call on" as: "...very degrading, really...because you was sort of pleading with the foreman to take you on." Bernie Bannister remembered how the foreman's favour was bought with a pint of beer: "Men – pubs were their way of life, because that is where the jobs was bought and sold. I was a kid then, in the *Millwall Dock Tavern*, and I see these jobs bought and sold", and Frank Soper, who was a foreman ganger himself, related how: "I come in when the pubs were shutting of a night. You go and do a day's work, you know what I'm talking about? Three or four hundred ton of stuff a day, you wanted your wallop before you come home. Come home drunk. She never used to say nothing. Cook me grub the next morning and away I would go to work again that day and come home drunk again. Yeah."

As a result of the high rates of poverty and unemployment, there were always men chasing the labouring jobs in the docks. Being so plentiful, they were not highly valued, and little was done to provide basic comforts and amenities, as Joe Waters recalled:

"There was nothing really ever done for improving the conditions of the men that were actually doing the work. And in the winter, in the toilets, it was terrible. As soon as you walked in, whether it was winter or summer, you more or less had to put a peg on your nose for the smell. That was one thing. They were always very very damp, the plumbing was a lot to be desired, there was hardly any locks on the doors. Once you were inside, the WC, hardly any toilet paper whatsoever. Cold water to wash. And nowhere to dry your hands in those days."

One group of port workers was even more steeped in tradition than dock workers and these were the watermen and lightermen of the River Thames. Admission to these high-status trades was by seven-year apprenticeship, usually handed from father to son. Dennis Dawson, whose father was a waterman, described his work:

A "Lighterman" is the man who controls a large river barge or lighter into which cargo is unloaded from the ship. He controls and steers the barge by means of two large oars or "sweeps". The sweeps are hefty things and it needs a lot of skill to operate them. The "Waterman" assists in the docking and berthing of the large cargo and passenger ships. As the boat comes in, he has to row his small boat to the ship. He then has to take a mooring rope from the ship, load it into his boat and row it to the dock where the dock hands take it and place it round a bollard at the berth. The ship then uses its winches to haul itself into berth, snug and secure and ready for unloading. Sometimes my Dad would take me with him on the jobs he was doing. Wherever we went people would stop to talk to him. Sometimes he would do dock

Discharging potatoes on the north quay of the West India Docks in 1948.

piloting and that meant he would be up on the bridge of the ship to pilot it out of the docks."

Mr Hiles emphasised the hard work and danger: "My mother had six brothers and five of these were lightermen as was my grandfather. These five uncles pulled their guts out almost, whilst wrestling their barges along the Thames, aided by a sweep that was long and heavy. They knew the Island only too well. It was a tricky job getting round that bend with a load of timber from Lenanton's; the fear of shipwreck always loomed."

Accident rates were high in the port – nationally, only miners were at greater risk. The poor working conditions, the casual system and the low pay that went with it were the main causes of industrial action by the port workers in the inter-war years. Their great champion was Ernest Bevin, who tried for twenty years to achieve registration, a minimum wage and the end of the casual system. When he became Minister of Labour in 1941 he was able to introduce some reforms, but it was not until well after the Second World War that any real improvement was made in working conditions for dock labourers.

Bernie Bannister mentioned the boats berthed in Millwall Docks. These included vessels from Stockholm Oslo and Copenhagen, with timber, general cargo and passengers on board. Besides the Swedish Lloyd, 15 other lines used Millwall in 1935, including boats from Russia and the United States. Nineteen further shipping lines used the West India and South West India Docks, including the Union Castle and Cunard Lines.

The total tonnage using the Port of London rose from under 40 million in 1909 to over 60 million in 1939; the percentage of Britain's sea borne trade handled by the Port rose from 29% to 38% and the number of dockers fell from 52,000 in 1920 to 34,000 in 1937. The increased business was partly a result of modernisation, which included the cuttings linking the West India, South West India and Millwall Docks, opened in the 1920s, a new Customs Baggage Hall at Tilbury Dock opened in 1930s for the thriving passenger trade, the appearance of the *London Mammoth*, the 150-ton self-propelled floating crane, and other improvements to the docks, of which the George V, opened in 1921, was the newest.

The fall in manpower reflected the introduction of conveyor belts and electric cranes which reduced the amount of labour required to shift cargo. In spite of these changes most cargoes were made up in units which could be manhandled, with the exception of bulk commodities such as grain and coal. Until after the Second World War the rapid turn-around required for steam ships was achieved by gangs of men working hard and fast for long hours to complete the unloading and reloading.

Rope had many uses amongst the ships, cargoes, barges and cranes at the docks, wharves and ship-repair yards from Tower Bridge to Tilbury. Supplies of Manilla fibre from the Phillipines and sisal from East Africa, Mexico and Brazil, were readily available. Hawkins and Tipson, established in East Ferry Road in 1881, had begun to make its High Grade Hercules Brand Manilla Rope in 1918, specifically to be used for towing oil barges and this led to orders from the expanding oil companies and from maritime markets around the world. When the Millwall Extension Railway closed in 1926, Hawkins & Tipson bought the land, demolished most of the thirteen arches of the viaduct and had new warehouses and office block erected. In the 1930s this enterprising company developed a waterproofing process for sisal ropes, creating a profitable new line of business.

The original family firm had become a limited company in 1919 and at the same time introduced a

Stanley Potter, under-manager at Hawkins & Tipson's rope works, with coir rope. This was "really rough stuff" used round the edge of lifeboats. The photograph was taken at the gateway of the works in East Ferry Road. Mr Potter is holding a sample of nylon rope, which was pioneered by this company.

profit-sharing scheme for their employees whereby 15% of profits was paid out to workers over the age of 18, in proportion to their wages. This was one of the first of its kind in the UK and was only abandoned in the Second World War. There was a sickness benefit club and later they introduced a pension scheme. This company had employed women ever since it was founded in 1881; they operated machines in the spinning mills. In 1938 new "dining and rest rooms" to quote the *East End News and London Shipping Chronicle*, were opened, fitted with a radiogram, wireless set, and two electric clocks. Here, as in most places, the workforce let their hair down once a year, watched in awe by local children: "We lived opposite Hawkins & Tipson's rope factory and on Christmas Eve when they had a party we used to stand at the window and watch the staff go rolling home, sober people all the year!"

As long as the port was busy, so were the ship repair yards, although employment varied with the number of ships in dry dock and the type of work to be done. Conditions here, as almost everywhere, were noisy, dirty and dangerous. William Chapman described his work as a boy of 14 at Green Siley Weir's ship repair yard, in the 1920s:

"I was interviewed by a bloke named Jerry. He was the charge-hand "carrier". Carriers were the

The Cutty Sark in dry dock at Limehouse, in the yard of Fletcher Son & Fearnall. The photograph was taken in 1920 by George Henry Wright, who worked there as a plater.

blokes who heated the rivets on the portable forges to white-hot heat under piecework conditions. Their skill and timing was fantastic. A good carrier was eagerly sought after, because the whole squad relied on each other as a team. They used to have usually five rivets in the coke at one time, and each rivet was moved to the centre of the fire in rotation according to the size required in their correct order, for example, at a join where two different thicknesses were encountered.

There were five in a squad. Two hand riveters, the holder-up, carrier and rivet boy, me in this case. My job was to keep my carrier supplied with rivets from the stores and bags of "breeze" for him to catch the white-hot rivet by the head at the angle of about

forty-five degrees. He then inserted it in the hole so that the holder-up could smack his big hammer against it without delay. The carrier used to drop the rivet down a steel pipe into a bucket of sand if you were working in the bowels of the ship.

The worst job was working in between the blocks that the ship rested on. There was about four feet of head room for crouching and knocking up these big inch and one-eighth diameter rivets. I have seen them with hands bleeding after eight hours continuous work. Tea breaks weren't allowed. It was instant dismissal if one was caught with a can of tea. These restrictions were gradually lifted, but until they were, we boys had to sneak away to the off-licence, buy a quart bottle of beer and get back without being seen."

Companies supplying construction materials to both home and export markets flourished. Two of the Island's major engineering firms were J.Westwood & Co., and Matthew T. Shaw. Shaw's was established in 1846 as fabricators of bridges, girders, roofs, sheds, forgings, etc. The premises consisted of two yards, one on either side of Westferry Road near Chapel House Street. C.M.Howard worked for 47 years in the design office and described the routine and some important contracts.

"The basic raw material (rolled steel sections in my day) was bought in from rolling mills in the north and stored in the stock yard. It was then cut, drilled, bolted riveted (or later, welded) to form the beams, stanchions, girders or roof trusses required for a particular contract. The sections were then painted, marked and inspected before being dispatched to various building sites around the country to be put together by steel erectors.

In the late 1920s and early 1930s we were contracted for the fabrication and shipment of several tin dredgers for re-erection in Malaya. They were for the mining companies there. Each contract was for a large floating dredger with superstructure to carry a long girder-type support for a bucket dredger. The machines dredged their way up in the Malay marshes, dredging for tin on the way and were finally abandoned, their work having been done. A similar job was carried out for a silver mine in Cyprus, in this case a complete steel-framed structure to form a large workshop.

Closer to home there were two interesting jobs of roof restoration. One was at Gloucester Cathedral, where a new steel truss roof was supplied and erected over the existing stone vaulting to replace the original timber. The other, a longer and more complicated contract, was carried out to the roof of Eton College Chapel.

All the work in the firm's yards was very heavy and overhead cranes were necessary to handle the material, so with these cranes, drillers, saws, riveters, all going full pelt the racket was considerable, added to which there was much rust and rolling mills oxide

Lorries and drivers outside John Lenanton's timber yard, Westferry Road.

under foot, making the process rather a dirty one, hence the platers' overalls and sacking aprons."

Westwood's, on the Island since the 1850s, had also supplied many overseas customers with iron and steelwork. After the First World War, the firm extended its range to all forms of fabricated steelwork, including steel frame buildings, mechanical grabs, light sheet metal equipment and an extensive steel stock-holding service. Many of Westwood's orders were for the home market, supplying the expansion of the road and rail network and the extension of the London Underground.

Westwood's had a large site in Westferry Road adjacent to Burrell's Wharf, and the very large girders in which the firm specialised created severe problems. Until the Blitz Westferry Road was lined with houses and shops, allowing little room for large lorries to manoeuvre in and out of the works' gateway with long loads. Added to this, the frequent "bridgers" at the docks caused frustrating delays. Sometimes the lorries laden with girders were too heavy for the old dock bridges to bear and the lorries had to pass through the dock area and on by specially planned routes, avoiding awkward spots.

Le Bas Tubes, at Cyclops Works in Westferry Road, was a company which handled metal tubes and malleable fittings. Close by were two other well-known Island companies, Brown Lenox, the cable makers, and Samuel Cutler's, where gas holders and

other large steel structures were made.

Lenanton's timber wharf had been on Batson's and Regent's Wharves in Westferry Road since 1837. It had supplied the great Thames shipyards when their trade was busy. Subsequently it supplied the ship-repair yards and in the inter-war years orders came increasingly from the expanding construction and furniture industries. Imported timber from all over the world was stored here, as well as English oak and elm. In the early 1930s the firm extended its site to include an adjoining wharf which had once been a dry dock, creating a total storage space of three-and-a-half acres. The great stacks of timber under the open sheds on the wharves were a noticeable landmark from the river for many decades.

Colour and paint manufacturers, Burrell's, was another success story of the period. In World War One, their export cargoes had been sunk by enemy submarine action and markets were lost as other countries manufactured for their own needs. There was also a shortage of raw materials. However, many Government contracts were secured and the engineers' shop was largely turned over to the manufacture of munitions.

As the aniline dye industry had been largely under control of German manufacturers, there was every incentive to develop the manufacture of pigments and dyes in Britain, and this is what Burrell's did. Colour-making increasingly became dominant in Burrells, though the production of paint remained important. Another colour-making firm in Old Ford was bought out in 1920 and in 1924 Barnfield Works was erected on the other side of Westferry Road, about 400 yards away from the main factory, solely for the manufacture of Organic Reds.

Expansion continued with reconstruction work on the Millwall site and the purchase of Savill's Brewery at Stratford for conversion into another manufacturing plant. Although the 1920s' slump affected Burrell's order books this was partly offset by a continued growth in the manufacture of chemical colours, for which there was an increasing demand in new industries such as plastics, cars and electrical goods. Burrell's employed many women and girls.

Another company which successfully survived World War One and the depression was Snowdon Sons and Company, manufacturers of lubricating oils, established on Millwall in 1891. Like Burrells they depended on a German product for their basic raw material, in this case an industrial grease and so had to start making their own during the First World War. As a result of the Russian Revolution in 1917 they lost an important customer and also had to write off thousands of pounds of bad debt. The firm survived the slump of the early 1920s, partly due to continuing demand in the export market, supplying the Near East, India, Sudan and Malaya amongst others. In 1933 the firm amalgamated with London Lubricants Ltd., and soon afterwards developed a new and very successful product, an engine oil containing detergent additives.

Locke Lancaster & W.W. & R.Johnson, or Associated Lead, specialised in refining and processing at their Westferry Road works, which employed around 300 people at its peak, including a number of women in soldering and in the paint section.

Millwall families visiting men from Cutler's steel works at Welwyn Garden City, where they were erecting gas holders and living on site in wooden huts. Left to right: Mrs Till Cox, Mrs Lizzie Thomson, Mrs Sophie Anderson, Harry Anderson (behind flowers), Kate Camm, her husband, and Fred Cox; Cox boys in front.

It was very busy in 1928 when J.Younger joined the firm as a laboratory assistant:
"...the lead factory was working all round the clock with day and night shifts. We would receive samples from all the furnaces and melting pots twice daily." He descibes the test conditions as "smelly, cough provoking and, often very dangerous and altogether unpleasant."

The company had a reputation for being considerate employers. Mr L.Jones, their chemist for many years, saw "old boys, the old employees of the company, coming to collect their pensions on a Friday morning, and that was in 1917, long before it became statutory. And the men got holidays with pay, unheard of." Frank Conn, who worked there as an office boy, also remembered that: "At Christmas, all the staff were given a turkey in a straw bag...our family had never tasted turkey up to then." There was also an annual outing to Margate, and a Christmas dance in the Glengall Road Baths, "where they put a wooden floor over the pool for dancing."

The wooden floor over the swimming pool may have been provided by J.F.Ebner, flooring specialists, of Stewart Street. This firm supplied wood block and strip wood floors all over the country. Many new public buildings were fitted by Ebners, who used beech, maple, oak, mahogany and the lesser-known Australian woods, jarrah and karri. The firm had its own wharf, kilns for drying, and mills for sawing, planing and making tongued and grooved strips. On the adjacent wharf was Stuart's Granolithic, a company which imported marble and stone for cutting and shaping.

The arrival of the motor vehicle revolutionised transport. Horse-drawn vehicles did not disappear until after the Second World War but there were a number of motor transport firms on the Island, often combining storage with the carriage of goods. In 1936 Poplar Chamber of Commerce welcomed the coming of the motor vehicle as an improvement on the traditional methods of rail transport combined with horse-drawn carts: "...door-to-door delivery... obviates the need for more handling at each end, reduces the risk of damage and removes opportunities for pilfering..." The writer also noted that special cattle trucks and horseboxes were keeping animals off the tarred roads when in transit to shows, markets, etc., and that the distribution of perishable foodstuffs – milk, fruit, vegetables and fish in particular – had been much improved by the use of the motor lorry .

Mr Huish had been a Regimental Sergeant Major in the Royal Engineers and was discharged in 1918 with chronic bronchitis. His wife was, in her son's words: "an equally strong and indomitable woman", who during the hard years of war, "had saved money for the time when he would return to make a new life." The family lived in Johnson Street, not far from the drawdock.

The story goes on: "After the Armistice, the army started to dispose of surplus equipment at Slough, and my father obtained one five ton Daimler lorry and two Harley Davidson motorcycles – these were new and in cases ready to assemble. Thus began his career as a haulier."

Customers were found particularly amongst builders, such as the local firm of Griggs & Son, "who had extensive contracts for office building and the building of houses...indeed they were responsible for work in Regent Street and other large London properties." As the firm expanded, "work was found with a ship's stores supplier, and transporting large quantities of road-making materials to local councils in south London; materials was also transported to local railway depots for onward transit..."

Davison's was another company which successfully managed the transition to motor vehicles, initially buying up old army lorries for conversion.

Lorry-driving was an exciting new skill which could be quite easily acquired by an ambitious youth. Veteran driver Jack Rump recalled: "I got in with John George's...and they had a whole fleet of lorries, that was a Ford on solid tyres, that was a Pearce Harrow on solid tyres, and a little Leyland and that had pumped-up tyres that one. Well, I wasn't a driver then but when I was 17, John George's asked me if I would like to drive for them, when I got 17. Oh, I said, I wouldn't mind because I was interested in lorries, like, all motors, and the day I was 17 they bought me my first licence what I have got here, they bought it, that's a blue licence, 1928, they paid five shillings for it, I'm sure they were five shillings then. And that was the first lorry I ever drove, a Ford, pumped up tyres at the front and solid tyres at the back ."

The restructuring of family firms into limited companies, combined with the take-over of rivals, or being taken over by rivals, was a common pattern in this period. Confectioners C. & E. Morton employed dozens of women and girls in making sweets and other foodstuffs, and they had two factories on the Island, one at the northern end of Westferry Road and the other in Manchester Road. After the First World War, Morton's lost much of their overseas market to new factories in the colonies. This affected the firm badly as they had produced almost exclusively for export. During the worst of their troubles, in the early 1930s, a new manager was

Lead foil department, Millwall lead works, 1930s. Lengths are being soldered to form a continuous roll for damp courses - the lead strip would be sandwiched between layers of bitumen. Lead sheeting was also used at one time to line tea chests, because it was impervious to air and moisture. Chemist Mr L. Jones recalled that the works supplied India, Assam, Burma and Ceylon with all the lead sheet they needed. Later, aluminium was used instead.

Alice Parmenter and Bill Hickman at a Masonic dinner in Holborn in 1938. The Hickman family lived at 135 Mellish Street. William Hickman senior ran a haulage business with his three sons; they also took charabanc outings to Margate and Southend.

brought in, whose drastic staff cuts provoked a strike. Mrs Perfect said: "We were out for a fortnight, getting no money, as we didn't belong to a union... In the end he had to have us all back, because there was no one to set the machines up... He didn't reign for very long." Eventually the company decided to move into the home market and in 1938 Morton's products began to appear in shops in England. Unfortunately for them the Second World War, with its rationing and restrictions on imports, put potential expansion on hold. In 1945 the controlling interest in Morton's was acquired by the Beecham group.

With changing markets, changing products and companies becoming larger and more powerful, many smaller firms found competition very intense. Price-cutting to keep customers led inevitably to efforts to reduce labour costs, either by reducing wages or by increasing productivity, or both. At George Clark's Broadway Works in Alpha Road, a

Loading up deliveries at George Clark's Works in Alpha Road, 1930s.

multitude of special sugars were produced for the brewing industry. There had been thousands of small breweries, but in the 1920s and 1930s, the number shrank to just seven hundred, all more price-conscious in their purchasing policy. Clark's struggled to survive. A staff of just 50 produced 8,000 tons of brewing sugar in 1939, but the outlook was poor if current trends continued.

Some companies went out of business or were absorbed into others. When George Thurgar's father came back from the war: "He found a job at the Glengall Iron Works, as a chauffeur. They used to do ship-repairing, iron manufacturing and components for ships. Then in the 1920s, there was a big financial scandal, it ruined a lot of firms, including Glengall Iron Works, that went bust and he was out of work," The Poplar Copper and Brass Works of George Brockley and Company, in Chipka Street, were taken over in 1939 by Messrs John Downton & company of Pennyfields, though all the workers were retained.

Dick Waterhouse's memories of jobs he did as a young unskilled labourer illustrate the shifting nature of employment and describe conditions which can hardly be imagined, let alone tolerated, in the 21st century. Here he recounts his experience at F.C.Giddens' cattle-cake mill, on Alpha Wharf:

"I went to the firm and got a job from a pompous individual whose attitude was like he believed he was doing me a favour. "Yes, we are taking workers on" he said, and when I heard that the pay was thirty-five bob for sixty-hour weeks of alternate night and day shifts I realised I had been "taken on" all right... When I turned up to begin my first spell of night work I was pleasantly surprised to see Larry Thompson and George Hook who both lived nearby...they were sociable and friendly and that was a bonus when I went to work with their gang.

I had worked on numerous job's since leaving Maconochie's as a van driver's assistant, most of them for firms whose work was of a seasonal nature or where a large order had to be completed in a given time – all of them lasting only for short periods. This latest job with a firm of cattle food manufacturers lasted from September 1928 until April of the following year.

The prospect of working long twelve hour shifts of night work every other week was not an ideal one. Working conditions were really grotty, the whole building was jam-packed with material, the stowage space included the only staircase linking the three floors with barely room to squeeze through. What would have happened in the event of a fire nobody gave a thought. There wasn't a messroom and the only means of making tea was by hanging a can over a gas jet on the lavatory wall or placing it just inside the boiler fire-box which was a quicker method except that if you left it too long the water would evaporate and the can would disappear up the flue.

I was sixteen and the others were around that age too, so it was hardly likely that any of us had had much experience if any, of working nights. At first it was a novel experience...the reality of course was seemingly endless spells of constant work and when a stop was made for a tea break it was always a struggle to keep awake....when work was resumed it always felt harder and when the pressure was increased for no other reason than the chargehand's wish to outdo the other shift's performance we sometimes were obliged to slow things down. We achieved this by adding some "foreign bodies" to material being fed to the pulverizer machine."

The strongest trade unions were those of the skilled occupations such as the boilermakers, the shipwrights and the engineers. Workers doing general labouring jobs in the Island's factories were unlikely to be organised, whilst people in low-paid, casual employment did not have the same rights to unemployment and sickness benefit as those in full-time skilled work. Dick Waterhouse, a radical thinker at seventeen, recalled how one of his older workmates "went pale with anger" at what he saw as young Dick's presumption in suggesting that they should have better sick pay and conditions. "It's not for the likes of us", was his response, when Dick pointed out that as things stood, they could hardly afford to be ill.

As well as the big and small companies with a full work-force, there were dozens of small, family run or "one-man" operations. These outfits, most of which would not merit a mention by Poplar Chamber of Commerce, ranged from builders and shop-keepers to window cleaners and street traders.

Shopkeeping was a family affair more often than not – sometimes women and older children ran the shop whilst the men in the family went out to work. Joe Leeds and his wife and daughters had a grocery shop at 88 Stebondale Street from before the First World War until the Blitz. Joe was able to invest the modest profits, mainly in shares in wholesale grocery concerns, and retired before the Second World War to a house in Catford.

Mr Gleeson was the manager of the varnish department of a paint firm in Stratford. He had to give up his job when he contracted TB. He had no sickness benefit as he hadn't paid his stamps, but he was a Freemason and he had a grant of £60 from them. With some of this capital he started up a little shop opposite the *Lord Nelson* pub, at a rent of seven shillings and sixpence a week. This was in the 1930s. He decided to sell socks and silk stockings – having four daughters he knew about the market for the latter. His daughter Maggie helped him and collected stock from a warehouse in Houndsditch.

Not everyone could get a job or keep a shop and periodic unemployment was a fact of life for many men during the inter-war years. Various ways were found to make a shillings here and there, one of which was recalled by George Pye senior:

"In the 1920s the drawdock was used by a couple of watermen, Mr Turner and Mr Brown, to break up old barges which had become useless by age and were unseaworthy. I understand the local Council had given them permission to use part of the shore for this, providing one half was kept clear for public use by watermen and others. Their labour force was the local unemployed lads, of which I was one. They also had the yard opposite the "shore" as it was called. They had all the gear kept here for barge-breaking, including crow bars and a kind of pick-axe called a mallet. All this gear was loaned to the lads for free. Their reward was the wooden skin of the barge which would sell as firewood for about five shillings a barrow-load. Brown and Turner would have the best part of the barge, the ceiling planks, metal bollards and pumping gear. They also encouraged the local children to scavenge the shore for the nails and nuts and bolts that were knocked out of the carcass, loaning them pails which the children then filled and took over to the yard to old Ferdani,

Albert Hall, a widower, kept a little shop at 13, Harbinger Road in the 1930s. His sister-in-law, Mrs Webb, had a haberdashery and off-licence in Westferry Road and supplied him with stock. He also sold from door to door and went round busking with his banjo.

their odd-job man, who would then weigh them and give them a couple of coppers. How's that for labour relations? Their barge broken up, a nice clean shore and all at no cost. In the late 1920s or early 1930s, I'm not sure which, Mr Calder, the Wharf owner next door to the railway yard, applied to take this over and also Johnson's Drawdock, but the local people were "up in arms" about this. So the Poplar Borough Council called a public meeting and it was agreed that the Drawdock was to remain a Public Drawdock for all time."

"It absolutely destroyed people to be unemployed" recalled one Islander.

Charlie Williams and his young wife had not been married long when his regular work, which had given them the courage to take to matrimony, unexpectedly dried up:

"I was out of work for nine months except for the odd few days I could get in the docks. All the lads were in the same boat. It was very demoralising but it didn't get us down. We all mucked in where possible and helped each other out. I used to give some of them hair cuts or mended boots when they bought the leather. I also helped Dad on the allotment. We tried everything under the sun to obtain a few bob from painting people's door knockers for a penny to pushing a coster "barrer" to Charing Cross for a local stall holder, buying a case of Dutch bulbs for ten shillings and selling them for eighteen pence a dozen for him in Roman Road market. I was told where I could obtain a gross of packets of assorted seeds at a Nursery in Catford. They were the equivalent of those that were sold in Woolworth's for tuppence a packet, but without the labels. So I went over and got a gross for sixpence and I made a few coppers out of them."

Ivy Kneeshaw's father Bill Woods was a painter and decorator, working for Mr Baker, the builder in Maria Street. His hobby was putting together old bikes which he painted and hired out for tuppence an hour from their back gate in Cheval Street. Bernard Thomas's father was another painter and decorator and ran and played in a dance band as well, both for pleasure and extra income.

The "tosher" like the mudlark of old, made a living collecting driftwood from the shore at low tide. Oddments of Scandanavian deal, Norwegian spruce, British Columbian pitchpine and other woods, fell off badly-laden barges or was dropped during handling, and could be gathered up, sorted and sold for home carpentry, repairs and firewood.

St. Mildred's Settlement helped the unemployed out in the 1930s:

"In 1934 some unemployed men came to dig the Settlement garden voluntarily. They asked if they might build a shed in it in which to occupy themselves, instead of idling away their days. The Warden got permission from the Port of London Authority to use a line of low rambling sheds bounding our garden and the docks. By the following

William George (Bill) Woods and Anne Woods, of 10 Janet Street, Millwall, on the occasion of their Golden Wedding.

year grants had been obtained, General Woodcock had come as Organiser and a local Committee had been formed. This Committee proved the means of establishing firm links between the Settlement and local firms...There were classes in boot-repairing and carpentry, lectures, debates and recreation. The Duchess of York,, now the Queen Mother, came to visit the men and the Club filled a very big need until, soon after the outbreak of War, it came to an end." John Hawkins was one Islander who remembered this club exactly as described above.

There were some signs of growth from the mid-1930s onwards. In 1935 the giant white silos of McDougalls Flour Mill rose up beside the Millwall Dock Outer Basin. They were to be a landmark for almost fifty years. In 1936 came the opening of Meyer's Subsidiary Timber Wharves Ltd, also beside the Millwall Dock. According to Harry Jenkins, who worked for the company from 1937 until his retirement, Montague Leveson Meyer: "...came down and spoke round the Millwall Central School, and they said they wanted to employ all local labour when they opened up. Which was a good thing. And he was quite a gentleman."

Islander Alf French recalls that by the middle of the 1930s, prospects had started to improve for everyone, not just those with ambition: "I mean, on the Isle of Dogs, what could you be, what could you do? Fortunately the City was growing and so by the mid-thirties there were quite good job opportunities

in the City, which with a reasonable education a young person could get. This is one of the advantages of having the commercial Central School... things were still quite grim, in the early '30s... and from 1935 onwards, things really did begin to improve, the docks improved, the chemical industries, everything, we were importing and exporting more, it was a good time for shipping, one thing gave stimulus to another and we certainly felt the advantage in East London, with people like Morton's the sweet factory, the sack factory and the various chemical works and the paint works, were all working overtime and this was something almost unheard of for the previous decade and of course then the workers were doing well on the strength of all this and it was offering new job opportunities for people coming from school."

3. Housing on the Island

When George Lansbury broke the ground with his spade to mark the start of building work on the Chapel House Estate, Isle of Dogs, in January 13th, 1920, he was opening up a new era in housing for the Island, the era of council housing. Over the next fifty years, the provision of good quality homes to rent from the local authority brought about a real improvement in living conditions for thousands of people across the UK.

Privately rented accommodation had provided homes for people of all social classes at the beginning of the 20th century, and continued to be used until well after the Second World War. Landlords derived a steady income from renting, and there were very few regulations governing the conditions they provided for their tenants. British Street (later Harbinger Road)

Backyards and gardens of old Millwall cottages in Westferry Road, in 1930.

Poplar Councillor George Lansbury cutting the first sod for Chapel House estate.

was part of the Charteris Estate until the 1950s. James Mee, who grew up there, reflected on the relationship between landlord and tenant: "Of course, Charteris, he owned that old drum we lived in in British Street, see, that's another thing, the aristocracy then, who they were I don't know, they used to own all these old drums and they really lived on, they thrived on, other people's poverty, didn't they?"

Islanders who had the worst housing conditions were those living in parts of Millwall and along Westferry Road, where the oldest cottages and tenements had been built for the first industrial workers in the early 19th century, often on boggy ground and with only the most basic amenities. These dwellings, after years of neglect and in spite of the best efforts of tenants and local sanitary inspectors, had become almost uninhabitable, but were still occupied. In 1930, following on from the flood of 1928, a depressing picture was revealed in a survey of homes in Westferry Road. The following are typical extracts:

No.345, basement, man, woman and baby, man out of work and receiving £1.10s from the Guardians, landlord, Burrell, very wet walls and floors; ground floor, man and woman, very wet walls, first floor, man, woman and boy aged 10, daughter died of measles and pneumonia, man was crane driver at Westwood's,

lost job owing to illness in 1928, done up by tenants, ceiling mended by landlord, plaster falling on stairs, roof leaking, paper in strips.

No.218, in an "ante-room": two men, sub tenants, a very dirty, damp little room; 2 bicycles in room.

No.220: Five families in this house, a total of 11 adults, three babies and a four-year-old "very damp, plaster falling everywhere, yard paving, brickwork and pointing defective, sanitary inspector never comes, and there is one W.C. for all."

The survey also found that bugs, fleas and "big bold rats" were the constant companions of the people living in these houses.

James Mee described similar conditions:

"Next to *The Vulcan*, you used to go down and turn left and it was called Totness Cottages. I suppose there must be about thirty of these old tenements, they were three storeys high. Now each of those had three families in them, and one toilet, so even if they were living on the second floor you know, three storeys up, they still had to come down to that toilet. And there were a lot of rough diamonds there you know. And people brought up respectable families that turned out quite nice from there."

Some homes, although very basic, were bigger and better than those described above:

"I was born in Ferry Street, Isle of Dogs and I

lived in a terraced house, which was a two-bedroom accommodation. And we had no hot water. It was all cold, straight from the tap, any hot water had to be heated by kettle, or else, we had a copper, which was water heated by wood, paper and wood, underneath. Dad used to get it from boxes or any bits of wood he would see in the street, he would pick up, fetch home and chop it down.

We had an outside toilet. It was a flush toilet, but it was outside, so you had to come out of what you would now call a kitchenette, but we called it a scullery. You would have to come out of that and walk round the side of the house and then go into the toilet, in the dead of night, in the pouring rain, in the snow about a foot deep and you still had to go out there.

No bath, it was a tin bath hanging on the wall outside. You only had baths once a week. And the tin bath was usually brought in on a Friday evening and the water was boiled in the copper and then scooped out with saucepans or big bowls into this bath. We was lucky we had what they called a bungalow bath, which was a long thin bath, it was almost the size of a bath today. But a lot of people didn't have that, they just had a small oval bath and they sat with their knees up under their chin. And often when you had a bath, your mum or dad would get in after you, because it wasn't a matter of changing the water for anybody. And then when you had finished you used to have to carry the bath out with the water in and tip it outside down the drain, because there was no way of getting it out otherwise.

In what we call the living room we had a small kitchener, which was a small fire with an oven, and a hot plate on top where you always had a kettle of boiling water. It started with paper and wood and then filled with coal. But the cooking in the oven was absolutely delicious. And that was lit every morning.

We used to have a lean-to, where my dad had built a roof from where we went outside the scullery to the wall to the next house. And we done (the washing) under there and he did put a few lines up for mum and she could hang them in there." (Joan Webb)

This family had a two-bedroomed house to themselves. Many families shared a house. The six-roomed "airey" houses built in Cubitt Town in the 1850s and 1860s were easily adapted to multiple occupancy.

Connie Davey's experience was typical . She was born in 323 Manchester Road in 1923, the second of two girls. Her father, an electrical engineer, was Alfred North and her mother was Lilian Hammond. . "In the house, Grandpa North had the front downstairs room and the back ground floor room was lived in by my grandparents Hammond. On the next floor, the front

Emily and Elizabeth Bines with Ron Bines in 1931 at No.8 Tooke Street, Millwall; the house stood opposite The Islander pub.

room had Uncle Bill and Aunt Phil and the back room was a living room, upstairs the front was my parents' room and the back was our room with a curtain halfway across for my Uncle Chris (her father's younger brother). Downstairs, the room at the back of Grandad North was the kitchen, there always seemed to be a lot of people about, it opened to the back yard and the toilet, at the end of the yard was a fence that Dad often used to help us over to play in the Mudchute."

Johnson Street is now that part of Ferry Street

Agnes Clark outside her home at 120 Stebondale Street where she lived with her parents, sisters and brother, in the early 1930s. Agnes worked at Brown's Hotel. She married Michael Bradley and they moved to Leicester during the Blitz.

almost opposite Island Gardens Station. In the 1920s there were nine houses there and the Huish family lived in one of them:

"Three of the houses belonged to the Railway Company for use by their employees (on the Millwall Extension Railway), namely, the driver, the guard and the porter. The remaining six were owned by private landlords and the average rent was twelve shillings and sixpence per week. On the other side of the street lived an Italian family of mother, father, four sons and three daughters, who had migrated to England from Massa Carrara in Northern Italy prior to the First World War. Father and younger sons were employed breaking up barges on the drawdock and the others of working age worked in the local lead factory.

Next door to us lived a widow with three sons and a daughter. When the elder son was provoked by his brother, the air turned blue, and they had frequent rows. The walls of the houses were not very thick and every word could be heard.

In our house, which was next, lived two families – my parents and five children and another small family of relatives. One factor in all the disagreements that took place was the overcrowding which families had to endure at this time.

The next house to us had three families, numbering twenty adults and children and one can imagine the squalor...one of the families had only one room for father mother and three children to live and sleep and as this was at the top of a three-storey house, imagine the work entailed in trying to exist in such circumstances...the poor woman with young children and only one outside toilet to serve all the people in the house would occasionally wrap the children's excrement in paper and throw it from a

back window to be cleaned up later. Unfortunately the aim was not always accurate and it would sometimes land in our garden!"

Mr Huish described how his mother tried to combat the vermin with which they were all infested: "...after the Friday night bath would come the inevitable indignity of having one's head scraped with a small-toothed steel comb to eliminate any lice or nits which may have survived the effects of Lifebuoy or Sunlight soap. Should any survive the scrubbing and scraping, one's head would be subjected to a liberal rubbing with paraffin to kill any remaining nits, before shampooing with green soft soap. My mother put up a tremendous battle against the inevitable bed bugs. The beds would be dismantled and taken into the garden where they would be treated with a blow-lamp. The wallpaper was frequently removed and the walls disinfected with Flit, Keatings Insect Powder, and copious amounts of Jeyes Fluid. My mother, poor woman, was driven almost to distraction in her attempts to rid us of these awful pests, but all to no avail as any reprieve was only temporary."

Acute overcrowding caused problems which would not occur to us today. One Islander relates: "...being as we only lived in rooms, my Dad and the

Macquarie Way, part of Chapel House estate, about 1934. Some better-off families, like this one pictured here, were able to afford cars, this is a 1928 12-horse-power Morris with outward-opening windscreen. Alfred Kettle, in the bowler hat, was the principal clerk in the West India and Millwall Docks. With him are his wife Mrs Florence Kettle and children Ron and Ray.

rest of us had to stand outside in the street while the nurse delivered the baby..."

Alice Mileman lived with her parents and sisters in a flat over Clary's bike shop opposite Christ Church: "Mrs Clary was very strict and would not allow us children to enter the flat once we had left to play outside, so my mother used to tie a basket on a rope and lower it down from the window with anything we needed, such as a ball or a coat, or money if we did the shopping; then anything was put in the basket and taken up in the same way."

The housing shortage was a national crisis and it was one which the coalition government of Lloyd George was determined to address.

"Homes for Heroes" was the slogan which summed up the widely-held view that the men who had endured so much in the terrible battlefields should come back to a decent standard of living. For decades before the war it had been the policy of successive governments to leave the provision of housing largely to the free market. But in 1919, estimates of housing need in England and Wales were for 600,000 new homes and it was clear that only a major change of policy could go anywhere near achieving this target. An Act passed in 1919 brought in the era of state-aided housing. A Housing Manual issued by the Local Government Board provided detailed plans for generously sized, architect-designed family houses with gardens and internal bathrooms, to be built in a landscape laid out with winding roads and trees. A further Act of Parliament offered financial incentives to private builders for erecting low-cost housing for sale or rent.

While the Act was in force the newly elected Labour-controlled Poplar Borough Council wasted no time in using its powers to build a miniature "garden city" on the Isle of Dogs, using vacant land between East Ferry and Westferry Roads. In Chapel House Estate, the houses were generously proportioned and had living rooms, parlours, kitchens with water heaters, separate bedrooms and fixed indoor baths, as well as ample garden space. Others followed in Hesperus Crescent, Manchester Grove and Kingfield Street. To move out of older property into one of these new homes was "paradise" as Ruby Tomlin (nee Lovett) put it, recalling her family's move to Hesperus Crescent in 1930, although, she added: "the only drawback was that we backed onto a tyre factory called Tysons and so had a few rats but we got a cat and that helped."

There were not enough new houses for those who needed them and another option was to move away to the new London County Council estates being built in the 1920s in Becontree and Dagenham, where there were jobs at the Ford Motor Company. However, higher rents, the cost of travelling and the separation from supportive relatives and neighbours made such a change impossible for Islanders who were unemployed or on low wages.

Most of those who moved away during this time were skilled tradesmen and people with experience of running a small business, such as shop-keepers and publicans. Some of the better-off had already emigrated, before the 1920s, to private developments in East or West Ham, Plaistow, or to suburbs south of the river. Now the new LCC estates offered them another choice. Connie Davey, whose father worked in the Millwall Docks, recalled: "We moved to Becontree (from the Island) when I was seven (in 1930) but Dad continued to work in the docks for some years, first going by bicycle and then by motorbike".

In 1931 there were still 5,500 applications on the Borough Council's re-housing list. Since 1920 they had provided 1,282 homes, including 627 families who had been nominated for re-housing at Becontree, Dagenham and other estates. An article in the *East End News* in November 1933, discussing the recent survey of 173 houses on the Isle of Dogs and other investigations, concluded that one family in four in Poplar alone needed re-housing and the total requirements for new house-building was in the region of 9,000 homes. It was estimated that thirty thousand people in Poplar were living in overcrowded homes. One desperate measure which was considered by the Minister of Health in 1934 was to house the homeless in disused passenger liners moored in the docks, but this scheme was soon abandoned on grounds of cost.

By the 1930s the government had retracted somewhat on planning and spending for local authority housing. There was opposition to council house building at local level too. Responding to press publicity about "the slums of Millwall". a property dealer named Abbott circulated a letter to Government ministers, M.P.s and others. Entitled "The breeding pens of Poplar", the letter condemned "the thousands who never do a day's work", and "the laziest, filthiest creatures", who, he alleged, were living on the dole, gambling, drinking, going to the cinema and breeding, at ratepayers' expense. "It is," he wrote, "the filthy tenants who make the slums, put them into Buckingham Palace and in a month it would be a slum."

Treating this kind of outburst with the contempt it deserved, the workers at St.Mildred's Settlement, which was located amongst some of the Island's worst housing, determined to make improvements. They were active in local welfare, and they had first hand experience of the effect of poor housing on daily life, especially on the mothers of large families. They organised the survey of housing in Westferry Road referred to above and used the findings to raise funds for The Isle of Dogs Housing Society. Its members were drawn from amongst their rich and influential friends and families, some of whom came to visit the Settlement. At a meeting of Housing Society members in 1932 Princess Marie Louise reportedly described the Island population as: "the most

Mrs Emily Dodkin and her daughter Ivy in their new flat in St.Hubert's House, 1936. The family moved there from Manilla Street. The electric iron is plugged into the light socket, and there is an electric fire as well as a combined radio and gramophone made by two of Ivy's brothers, Tom and John. The family remained in these flats until the 1990s.

delightful and brave people, living in terrible conditions, courageously and without complaint..." whom she had come to know and love. With this and other support, the Society raised enough money to purchase land in Janet Street on Millwall. Old cottages were demolished and a block of flats, St.Hubert's House, was erected. It was opened in November 1935 by the then Duchess of York and Millwall families moved in.

Another private initiative was Jubilee Crescent, in Manchester Road, where the ship-repair firm, Green Siley Weir, built alms houses for its retired workers. These 30 flats were opened by the Duchess of Gloucester in 1937. The estate was later run by the East Thames Housing Association .

Meanwhile, the Labour-controlled Poplar Borough Council and the London County Council, remained committed to the provision of affordable, decent housing. But the post-war ideal of an architect-designed house with garden for every working-class family had been abandoned. Five-storey blocks of flats, each providing all modern amenities, sharing communal gardens, playgrounds and drying areas, had become popular and 40 per cent of London's subsidised housing between the wars was in flats.

Under the combined efforts of Poplar Borough Council and the LCC, blocks of flats were built all over the Island in the 1930s. They included Providence House in Emmett Street; Dunbar House in Glengall Road; the Kingsbridge Estate of three blocks on Phoenix Wharf near the Millwall Dock Entrance, named Montcalm, Montrose and Michigan after the Canadian Pacific steamers which had docked at Millwall before the First World War; the Westferry Estate in Westferry Road; and Roffey House and Cubitt House at the northern end of East Ferry Road. Some of the houses in the Island's oldest streets – Cuba Street, Manilla Street and Tobago Street – were demolished and 367 residents from 61 houses in Cuba Street, along with others, were moved to the new Westferry Estate.

Patrick McSweeney and his six brothers lived with their parents in an upstairs back room at No.16 Gaverick Street until with an eighth child on the way, they were allocated a three-bedroomed flat in Dunbar House for 12 shillings and sixpence a week. "They hired a coster barrow from the fishmonger, Harry Baggs and my Uncle Din, who was out of work,

Jubilee Crescent when first built.

New flats in Westferry Road.

moved our pathetic bits and pieces round to the new house and in doing so transferred all the bugs as well, so we still had itchy nights. But, at last, we had an indoor lavvy, a bathroom, a separate kitchen for cooking, three bedrooms and a front room. It was so palatial that for the first week we'd get lost, wandering from room to room!"

Not everyone approved of their new homes. Mrs Arthey of Spring Garden Place, Millwall, told the *East London Advertiser* in 1936 that she objected to flats because there was no garden, no drying ground of her own and nowhere for the menfolk to have a hobby. All she could do in a flat was to "look at her four walls".

Mrs Bennett, born 1909, was the seventh of a family of 12 children, who were one of the first families to move into Triton House, a new block of flats in Cahir Street. Here, they were allocated two flats due to the size of the family. These flats had an inside toilet and a kitchenette, which contained a bath "that had a lid", and an old-fashioned iron copper, "you had to light that up to have a bath, but nine times out of ten we used to go to the Public Baths, save all the inconvenience of lighting up fires." As the children grew up and the family got smaller, after the Second World War they moved again, this time into Warspite House, where "three lots of different people had to share a bathroom. Yes, three lots of families had to share one bathroom, that's where you had to do your washing, bathing and washing all in there."

For those who didn't want to share a bathroom, or for the many still without any kind of bathroom, bathing and laundry could be done in the Public Baths in Glengall Road (later Tiller Road). About 1934 the front half of the old building was demolished and a new building faced the road, incorporating Mens' and Ladies' Slipper Baths, office, boardroom (hired out for meetings) and accommodation on the first floor for the resident superintendent. At the rear of the building was the swimming pool and the public laundry where people brought their weekly wash, done in enormous machines. There were drying horses and an ironing room. A family wash took about three hours and cost one shilling and sixpence.

The newer homes built in the inter-war years gave tenants the benefit of electricity and hot water (and the extra bills to go with them). There were not many labour-saving devices and most people continued, like those in the old Victorian houses, to live much as their mothers and fathers had done – with basic furnishings and equipment. Joan Webb described domestic life in her Ferry Street home:

"My mum used to black-lead the stove and you could almost see your face in it. On our one we had a little bit of stainless steel on the edges which she used to polish up with emery paper, so that often was my job, to do that.

And our front doorstep was always done with hearth stone, that was a whitening agent. Wash the step down and then rub this on. They used to mix it with water and it was like a paint and it's a completely white step, as bright as a new pin when it's all done. If anybody stepped on it, you would go out and do it again, or my mum would, because she was so fussy.

And inside, there were no fitted carpets... they had loose mats, but we did have lino, which a lot of people didn't. A lot of people had hard work with the boards, scrubbing. We had lino and these loose mats and they used to be taken out and put on the line and beaten (with) the broomstick handle or the broom itself, give it a whack. The mats were the mats they made themselves, they was all cut out of the old coats and suits in thin strips, cut all the pieces up and they

Pier Head Cottages at Millwall Dock entrance.

Drawing by Frank Conn (brother of Albert), of his wife Sally and two sons Reg (standing) and Ron, in the kitchen of their home at 5 Pier Head Cottages, in the 1930s.

used to get a best sack, hessian, and pull it through and they used to go all over it like that and they used to make a mat and you used to back it underneath and that was all the mats that you had.

My mum did the washing every Monday which was most people's day and she would start in the morning with the sheets first, all the whites first. and they was put in the copper and boiled and then taken out and in the sink and rinsed and then taken out to a mangle outside which had great big wooden rollers. And underneath she would have another tin bath and that would be full of water with a blue bag in it, with blue rinse, so that would make the whites extra white. And I still buy blue bags today. And then they would be rinsed a few times and put through the mangle and you didn't iron the sheets, the mangle ironed the sheets. It used to be my job, she would fold them and then while she was mangling I would have to pull them so they didn't need ironing, the creases would come out. After the whites it was the towels and then the coloureds. And there was the rubbing board, because there was nothing, the copper, it was just hot water, there was no mechanism for turning it, you actually stood the rubbing board in the bath outside and then you rubbed up and down with a great big tablet of Fairy soap, rubbed the soap on, especially the collars and cuffs of shirts. And that was all done by hand.

Of course, you never had an ironing board, you used to do it on the table with a blanket and a table cloth on top. The only mixers you had was your own hands and for the beater you held the spoon or did it with a fork. Nothing electric like that at all. I can't even remember carpet sweepers until after the war. Everything was done with a broom and dustpan and brush. And we did have carpet on our stairs and on each stair she had a brass stair rod, which was polished every week.

4. Domestic and Family Life

Frank Conn wrote in his autobiography about a time when his father was out of work, and the family's benefit of one shilling a week was stopped because his mother refused to sell her cabinet gramophone: "...if it hadn't been for good family relations on both sides we would have starved, many a time Mum found a parcel of food on the doorstep, which we knew Grandad Conn was responsible for... Our Aunts, Mum's sisters, kept us clothed and shoes on our feet..."

Most people were reluctant to appeal to the hated benefits agencies or to charity. Family members would rather help each other out, knowing that the favour would be returned in time of need.

Neighbours also looked out for each other: "If my Mum made a rice pudding, there was a family I was friendly with, there were nine children in that family, if we didn't eat it all we used to cover it up and take it up to them...that sort of thing went on all over the Island. It was very close knit, very close knit." (Bill Boylett)

Circumstances varied between families, partly because of the different stages in the family life-cycle, partly because of varying levels of income. Poverty was felt most keenly when only one wage was coming in to feed and clothe small children, whereas a family which included several grown-up children working locally would be considerably better off. Mary Kingshott's family was like that in the 1930s, illustrating the variety of local employment:

"My eldest brother Tom worked as a stoker in Lenanton's timber yard; Fred worked at the rope works, Hawkins and Tipson, my sister Ivy worked there too. Rose worked in Maconochies on Pan Yan Pickle and Marie and I both worked at C. & E. Morton's until we were bombed out...My father was a waterman and lighterman working on the barges."

A family in which both parents were healthy,

Neighbours and friends in Newcastle Street (later Glengarnock Avenue) photographed during Coronation celebrations in 1937. Mrs Harris, Mrs Phyllis Hammond, Mrs Phyllis Steet, Mrs Worcester, Mrs Sophie Roberts, Mrs Morgan, and Annie Waters. The house was destroyed on October 17th, 1940.

Golden Wedding party for Louisa and Thomas Hoskins of 96 East Ferry Road, about 1930. The photograph includes many members of the Hoskins, Cole and Sutherland families, in-laws and grandchildren. All worked locally, Thomas Hoskins was an iron ship-builder and boiler-maker, Charles Hoskins was a barge builder, Frederick Cole was a docker.

hard-working, and good managers, was very different from one in which one parent was dead, disabled or unable to work, or where a high proportion of the weekly income was spent on alcohol or gambling.

One Islander recalled how men would get: "a couple of days work in the docks and they would come out and lose it all, more or less, in a game of Pitch and Toss".

Many recorded and written memories include evidence of those who "don't want to know", who don't wish to recall their Island childhood, unhappy years when their lives were made a misery by being an unpaid drudge to mother and younger siblings, by having to take adult responsibilities on too early; by having to beg from relatives, by having a father too fond of his drink, whose pockets had to be searched for odd coppers as he slept; through brutal physical punishment, through emotional or sexual abuse; through the loss of a mother, or both parents, and the consequent removal to a "home", which sometimes involved separation from siblings; through being constantly hungry and suffering from minor ailments, through having clothing more worn and ragged even than other poor children and wearing charity boots.

One Island woman said of the pre-war years; "They were horrible times. I know a lot of people say,

"Good old days" but not me, no definitely not, not for the way of life."

The less fortunate families served to remind others of the importance of mutual support within and between the many extended families on the Isle of Dogs, where groups of close relations were to be found living within a short walk of each other, and often in the same house. Bill O'Neill's family was one of these:

"I was born in the upstairs front room of 176 West Ferry Road in October 1927 in the shadow of Le Bas Tubes and under the sign "Cyclops Iron Works" where my father worked as a welder. I came from a large and complicated family background.

My father, Tom O'Neill, was born at 202 West Ferry Road. He had five older brothers: Jack, Mike, Patsy, Dan and Bill. They all served in the 1914-18 War. He had five sisters: Kate (who emigrated to American in 1926), Nell (who died young), Liz, Bridget and Mary.

My mother, Linda, was also born at 176 and lived there with her grandparents, Mrs and Mrs Ward, until their death. She carried on living there after her marriage.

Her mother, Rose, married George Marsh. He already had a son, George. They then had five children of their own: Bill (who died in 1926), Fred,

Flo, Rose and Mag. They lived downstairs in No.178.

Living downstairs in No.176 was Nanny Marsh's sister, Florrie, who married Jack Avis. They had three children, Fred, Florrie and Bill. So the three main family names were O'Neill, Marsh and Avis.

Bill Johnson, who worked most of his life at Levy Brothers and Knowles, the sack people, married my father's sister Liz. They had four sons, Tom, John, Jim and Ted and three daughters, Nell, Mary and Lizzie. They lived in Ingelheim Place and later in Becontree. Nell married my mother's brother Fred and they were one of the first families to leave the Island for Becontree. They had two daughters, Joan and Maureen and two sons, Tony and Jimmy.

Aunt Florrie Avis's son Fred married Ada Hutchings, whose brother Bill married Mary Johnson. They had two children Rene and Bill. So two more names were added to the family: Johnson and Hutchings. The Hutchings came from Poplar.

Other Island connections by marriage were my

mother's sister Rose who married Mick Webb of Stewart Street who was related to the Berrys; her sister Flo married Albert Dyer from Malabar Street. Albert's brother Bill was one of the three sailors from the Island to serve on *HMS Ajax* in the Battle of the River Plate.

Flo and Albert lived upstairs in No.178 West Ferry Road. My father's sister Nell married Jack Devlin from the Glengall Road area. They had two sons, Johnny and Paddy, and three daughters, Kitty,

A wedding uniting the Twiggs, of Claude Street, with the Wellers, of Plevna Street, in the 1920s. The groom was Arthur Weller, a docker, and the bride was Rose Twigg.

Eileen and Molly. Aunt Nell died when Paddy was a baby. Kitty lived with Nanny O'Neill, Paddy with Aunt Bridget (upstairs at No.202) and Molly and Eileen with their father.

Aunt Mary, my father's sister, lived with her husband Albert Whetton downstairs in No.204. They had two children, Edie (a girl) and Eddie (a boy).

Upstairs lived my mother's stepbrother, George Marsh, married to Aunt Mag. They had two sons, George and Reg, and three daughters, Rose, Olive and the youngest whose name I can't remember. They moved from there to flats in Cahir Street and later to Kidbrooke.

So a lot of my immediate relations were cousins, aunts and uncles at the same time and in consequence we used to have some large family parties."

John Breen, born in 1920 at 332 Manchester Road, also recalled overlapping networks of extended families in the immediate neighbourhood:

"The house was occupied by my parents, Jack and Jessie Breen, and my sister Jessie and me, and my maternal grandparents, George and Emily Mantle. My grandfather was a well-known local figure as he was coachman to Dr.Cardale and drove a large green and black Studebaker which was garaged behind Cardale's house in Glengall Road. Our neighbours to one side were the Radiczes, a stevedoring family of Scandinavian origin, and on the other side Mr and Mrs Collins, with Mrs Collins' mother, Mrs Hepworth, and her daughter and son-in-law, Marjorie and Jack Matthews and their son. Mrs Collins' sister, Mrs Easter, lived in the terrace near the bridge and one of her sons subsequently married my wife's sister.

Amongst the near neighbours in the rising numbers towards the bridge I recall the Devonshires, Clarkes, Cullens, Hooks and Whites; further up near the Co-op shop were the Wests and Hardings. The Griffith family lived across the road in the 500s. No. 531 was once Dr.Cardale's surgery and relatives of mine lived in the house and acted as caretakers. At a slightly lower number lived another aunt of mine, Mercy Rickman and her family; they were also related to the Hook family.

My mother's brother, Claude, a dock police officer, lived in East Ferry Road with his family, and other relatives were scattered around." (From *Memories of Childhood on the Isle of Dogs*, Hostettler (ed), 1994)

Marriage within the same area and the same social group was the main way in which these kinship networks came into being and sometimes bride and groom were already distantly related before they were wed, so that their marriage strengthened existing ties. A search of marriage registers for Christ Church revealed that of 100 marriages conducted there between 1936 and 1938, in only 13 cases did one of the partners (the groom) give an address which was not on the Island. The marriages in this Cubitt Town church were overwhelmingly between Island families. George Thurgar confirmed this pattern in the western side of the Island:

"It is remarkable really the Millwall families that married Millwall families. At that particular time it was virtually, well, more or less virtually unknown to marry somebody from miles away, they nearly always used to marry somebody that lived in the next street or a couple of streets away."

William Chapman and his girl friend Lilian Harrigan both grew up in "the blocks" in Mellish Street. They got engaged in 1929, when William, who was 21 and had already been at work for seven years, had got a job at "Gifco", the General Iron Foundry in Westferry Road.

"She was working in a factory close at hand and was earning 25 shillings a week for very hard and strenuous work. My wages weren't much. I had just enough left over for a few odds and ends and a weekly visit to the pictures. Lil had a troublesome and harassed life which had been her lot since childhood, so naturally the first opportunity to get married and live a life of her own was taken.

We were married at St.Luke's Church. Lil had found a couple of rooms in Alpha Road for eight shillings a week. I was flabbergasted at the amount of stuff she had acquired for our home out of the few meagre shillings she had left after paying her way and dressing herself. It was complete even to the tin opener. I know I had ten shillings which I spent hiring the local Rolls Royce which took us to the church and round to the pub for a drink."

Middle-class marriages were a different matter. When Rose Saulter married Philip Evans of West Ealing, her address was given as "Billson Street, North Greenwich", the newspaper report gave a description of elaborate dresses for bride, bridesmaids and mothers, and there were over fifty wedding presents including silver, cut glass, and furniture. The ceremony took place in a church in Ealing and the couple left for a honeymoon in Torquay.

Managing the domestic budget was a constant source of anxiety for most Island families, especially those with young children and where there was only one irregular wage coming in from casual employment.

"My father was a casual stevedore, a dock labourer who was employed for perhaps two, three or very rarely four days a week. His wages therefore over the twenty years he was on the Island were never more than two pounds and ten shillings a week. The rent in our council house was fifteen shillings a week, plus one shilling and sixpence for electricity. All the water for washing clothes, baths and cooking was heated on a gas stove, and a flat iron heated on the stove was universal – electric irons were a new invention in the 1930s. Sometimes the pawnbroker was the only way to overcome a difficult period, perhaps when Daddy hadn't had any work for a week. I well remember taking a pair of brand new boots to Squires, the Island pawn shop, and asking five shillings for them. I was offered three shilling and sixpence by the old gent behind the counter – which I just about reached with my arms stretched upwards. Everything we pawned was never, ever redeemed; that was the way of many a pawn bundle. At these times the rent money became overdue and I remember taking the rent book to the paying-in office in Poplar High Street. There I asked the clerk to take five shillings off the arrears plus one week's rent. He once said to me: "So long as your father keeps up the arrears payment, no action will be taken." I never told my father this. Another item in the weekly budget was the insurance; it amounted to sixpence a week and covered the deaths of both Mum's and Dad's parents. There was no social security system so this insurance was regarded as an evil necessity. Most of our clothes (if not home-made) were on credit and a tally-man would call on practically every house in the street to make a weekly collection. Perhaps once a month, Mum and Dad would have a "night out". This amounted to a walk through the foot tunnel to Greenwich where in the Express Dairy Dad would give Mum the treat of her life – a scrumptious dairy cream puff and a pot of tea, served by a smartly uniformed waitress. This would cost one shilling and sixpence."(Mavis Skeels, nee Taphouse)

Mr Huish recalled that the tally man would very often call for weekly payments when the husband was out. He knew that in many cases the husband was unaware of the debt, and he used this as a threat to get the next instalment paid. A piano could be bought for one shilling and sixpence a week.

There were several money lenders on the Island. George Thurgar described one as: "Rather florid-looking lady, they used to call her "Lobster" because she had a very red face, loads of gold rings and bracelets and what not, she was very opulent, more so than local people. They used to go and borrow off her and pay her back over a period of weeks or months or whatever it was…".

Savings clubs, Christmas clubs and clubs for specific items like boots did not involve getting into debt. Iris Barnes' mother, Carrie, ran a "shoe club" in Chipka Street. The fifteen members each paid one shilling a week. The numbers one to fifteen were written on slips of paper and each member took a slip. Whatever number they picked was the week they got a fifteen shilling token to spend on boots or shoes from Newell's shop in Chrisp Street. Carrie Barnes, as the organiser, was entitled to number one, but she seldom kept it, as there was always a member whose children were in desperate need of footwear.

Boots were sometimes provided by local businesses or charity. Joe Waters came from a large family in Stewart Street. "I can recall, as a boy, quite often not having any shoes and socks to wear and I can remember one Christmas very very vividly, whereby the Port of London Authority Police ran a

Christmas party, tea party for some of the children and instead of receiving a toy, or anything of that nature, what we did, we had to go to a boot and shoe

Joseph Squires was the Island pawnbroker and this is his old shop, which closed in 1965. Pawnshop "runners" took other people's goods into pawn for them, charging a penny a parcel. Lew Lloyds' milk shop, burnt out in the Blitz, stood to the right.

When Tom Clayden had a good job with the Metropolitan Gas Company, he and his wife Daisy could afford a week's holiday, with baby Tom, at Margate in 1924. When he gave up the job, the only holiday they had was hop-picking.

shop, in Chrisp Street, Newells, I believe, and we would get measured up for a pair of boots and when we went to the Christmas party, after we had our tea and cakes, whatever it was, sandwiches, before we left for home we were issued out with these boots, 'course we treasured those."

By 1921, the National Insurance scheme provided cash benefit for certain categories of workers in long-term unemployment, providing that they could prove they were genuinely seeking work and that they had no other means of support. "Means of support" was extended to include other household members in the early 1930s. Additionally, people could claim "Poor Relief" (renamed Public Assistance at the end of the 1920s), to top up existing benefits or to replace benefits which had run out. The "Means Test" caused a great deal of resentment.

"If you didn't have any money you used to be able to go on what you called the R.O, that's the Relief Office. And you used to go and plead with them to get money. Then if they did give you any money, they used to give you a Means Test. These officers used to come down and look over your house and if you had got anything in the house which you could sell, that's what you had to do. There wasn't much they left behind. They used to have chairs to sit on and a table, nothing else. And a bed. Towards the end of the 'thirties, it got more lenient."

Alf French described how living standards were beginning to rise in the 1930s: "...there were fewer and fewer being seen without boots and ties... and then nearly every child from about 1932, '33 onwards, had a tie at school... Because as the 1930s developed, rearmament and various other things, there was a greater degree of prosperity; more industries in London opened up and people could afford basics – they could afford clothes, shoes and that sort of thing. Gradually you did see children who were wearing ties and who were wearing socks and that sort of thing, and looking a bit smart, and gradually, you see, you wanted to be the same."

In addition to supporting poor families with cash benefits through the Public Assistance scheme, the government in the 1930s also encouraged local authorities to provide maternity and child welfare services and school meals. These provisions supplemented or took over existing agencies, such as those run by St.Mildred's Settlement and other religious bodies. In an effort to encourage better hygiene, the Council supplied free disinfectant, which had to be collected in glass bottles from a depot in Stebondale Street. This was a chore which children did, usually in return for a small tip.

Some people supplemented their income, or in certain cases, made their entire living, out of pilfering and other forms of petty crime. This was widely acknowledged and implicitly condoned. Here is an account of shop-lifting

"...the way she used to get away with things.

She'd fill her bag up almost. She'd fill her bag up almost, she'd have a big bag. She'd give him a lot of soft soap talk all the time. And every time he turned his back she'd snatch something and... put it in the bag. ...It was so much easier to steal because you knew there'd only be one stall holder... while he's serving people from that side you could rob him from – on this side he wouldn't know, he wouldn't know anything had gone. I stood there like that, looking... I couldn't say to the woman, "Oooh, the man's coming now" and I couldn't say to the man"that woman's put so-and-so in her bag" because she'd swear that she bought it."

The food, raw materials and finished goods which circulated in hundreds of thousands of tons through the Port of London acted like a magnet to the light-fingered poor. When asked if there was much stealing in the docks, Dot Bennett replied: "Ho! Not much! Rolls of cloth and materials and what have you." She added: "Plenty of smuggling in the docks. Used to see a policeman walking a man down the road and know he's come out of the dock. We knew who they (smugglers) were but we wouldn't say nothing. Didn't do to say unless you could prove it, in case they got into trouble. If I saw anything, I wouldn't say a word. I'd clear off out of it."

Alf Cottage related that if the draw bridge in Glengall Road was out of action: "people had to enter the docks to go over the locks, a woman took an empty pram in one entrance and came out the other side with a pig dressed in baby clothes and a bonnet on its head, of course her husband was a docky." This, he said, was a true story. He also described how a barge loaded with rolls of cloth and curtains, a hundred ton, and large reels of cotton meant for factories, "broke loose in the Thames and finished up in the cutting, when it became known the women unloaded it and dragged it home...new suits was all the go for years."

Other ways to make money go further were growing vegetables and rearing chickens or rabbits. Joan Webb remembered: "The garden was not a garden as such, it was just paved over with stones. We always kept chickens out there and a few rabbits. But we didn't like killing the rabbits because they became pets. We used to have chickens and set our own eggs as well, to get chicks. And then in the summer we used to grow our own runner beans. We always had a mint

The Lewis brothers of 18 Kingfield Street, about 1928. At the back, Arthur and Percy; in front Eddie and Ernie and Reg, the youngest until a sister Flossie was born. Their father Henry was a window cleaner and lamplighter and did other odd jobs. All the boys went to Cubitt Town School. Arthur became a milkman and worked at the lead works, Percy carried on the window-cleaning, Eddie and Ernie worked in the building trade and Reg was at Hawkins & Tipsons all his life.

bed, a great big mint bed of fresh mint out there."

Very careful spending was the bed-rock of the domestic economy. Joan Webb's recollections illustrate this:

"You ate everything everyday, you never kept anything. The only thing you kept was bread. If we was hungry, used to go in and get a couple of slices of bread, and then put dripping on it. You would have tinned condensed milk and cocoa. Cocoa would be in cardboard cartons because you would only buy a two ounce or four ounce, you don't buy in quantities you buy today. Nothing was really sold in quantity. What used to maintain us was, we had a kitchener, like a range, and my mum always used to buy what they called a penn'orth of pot herbs. Well, that was turnips, potatoes, carrots, peas, and make a big stew. And that was always on the fire range. So every time we came in we used to go and have a cup of soup with barley in it and everything.

We never seemed as though we ate so much as we do now. There was none of this in between, picking bits you know, chocolate biscuits. If you had chocolate biscuits you only went and bought two ounces. Biscuits was never stored indoors as they are today. My mum did a lot of cooking, she made a lot of cakes and pies, apple pie. And we used to have meat pudding a lot. Steak and kidney pie. But I was lucky."

Apart from cooking, the mother of a large family, like Mrs French with five boys and a girl, had a constant round of daily tasks to perform. After the children had gone to school the room was swept: "...sweeping was one of the big things in those days, you took all the mats up and you swept everywhere and it was all rather hard work especially when you had been moving coals out of the coal cupboard and the coal dust moved along the carpet." Then there was the daily shopping to do. Although a "big shop" was done in many families at Chrisp Street market on a Friday night or Saturday, small amounts of items required for daily use, or sudden needs, such as a box of matches or some vinegar, were fetched from local shops (which of course relied heavily on these small purchases). Then the dinner would have to be prepared and whilst it was cooking Mrs French would "...do sewing, there were always socks to darn and shirts to mend and trousers to patch" Dinner was served up and cleared away, following which Mrs French: "...dusted the mirrors and the glasses and pictures, did the beds, changed anything that had to be changed." Then on certain days she might have an hour's rest before at four o'clock: "...she was up again and preparing things for tea, and getting things ready for the evening... it was a continuous job". The week's programme included major tasks such as Monday's washing: Tuesday was the day for ironing; on Saturday there was the weekly shop at Chrisp Street – by bus and on foot, carrying heavy bags, and on Sunday the

highlight of the week, the Sunday lunch, to be cooked with careful management of the kitchen range. (Alf French)

Meanwhile babies and any children too young to attend school had to be cared for. In the evenings there might be more mending to do, and this is also when fathers repaired boots: "... we always had to repair our own boots, we never sent them along to the shoe repairer, he used to keep a supply of leather and he kept a whole box of nails and they would be repaired..."

Many housewives, occupied like this, had no time for anything outside the home. Some, with smaller families, or whose families had grown up, were able to go to work to supplement the household income, but in such cases they often worked only seasonally, at the jam factory, for instance. Others earned a few pence by taking in washing, taking in ironing, acting as "nurses" to women after childbirth, being "pawn shop runners", selling home-made toffee from their front room or otherwise finding a minute niche somewhere in the crevices of the local economy. Mrs Ramage, who lived in Stewart Street, "did washing for people in the old-fashioned copper in the yard"

Alf and Daisy Payne, with their daughter Myra (later Thomas) of Manchester Road, 1930.

46

according to her daughter Elizabeth, who was sent with a pushchair to buy wood at threepence a sack from Ebners, who made floors.

Lodgers helped with the rent but could be a mixed blessing. Privacy was impossible, since anyone living upstairs had to come through the downstairs living-room to reach the cold water tap and the toilet in the back yard. Sometimes lodgers were single individuals – unmarried men, or elderly people. Lodgers as married couples or small families often had even less space than the family with whom they shared; they had no amenities except a gas ring to cook on, and the resultant tensions often led to arguments. Alf French described the lodgers in his childhood home as "...an old lady and her two sons (who) didn't seem very keen on their girl-friends, they seemed much more keen on their pigeon racing and horse-racing and invariably spent a lot of time in the local pubs coming home terribly drunk and... there were times when we had to send for the police because of terrific fighting going on, the ceilings downstairs would crash as they hurled each other to the floor and crockery was broken..."

Constant anxieties about work and money, combined with the fact that most parents worked hard all day, left little time to play with children. Children played with each other, and parental intervention in their lives was confined largely to general care – feeding, clothing, etc., and to discipline, which was strictly enforced in many homes. Children were expected to be polite and obedient and to help around the house:

"Dad was strict and so was mum, I mean she used to have us there and line us up and daren't have a speck on our shoes, we had to spit on our shoes of a night and watch them in case there was any scratches on them and then we used to line up and if anyone had a chip off their shoes they used to get a hiding for that. Oh yes she was very strict and so was dad. Couldn't answer 'em back. None of us couldn't answer 'em back otherwise you'd get the strap. You had to be in a certain time....like when I started courting and take him home, no way, we used to get to the corner there and he used to say, It's about time you were in. I never went courting till I was nearly nineteen then I went with him for eight years before I got married."

Most children had to learn the facts of life for themselves:

"Did parents ever talk about sex with their kids?" "No." That was one account, but another elderly Islander recalling his youth, said:

"I met a lot of girls, me and my mate and if we came home of a night time and we hadn't escorted two young ladies home or spoken to them, there was something wrong... We was disappointed... So in my life I took girls home... (but) always kept away from sex. You had your usual cuddle and kiss, but I was always afraid of diseases and that. And I think a lot of us was. Because they kept pumping that into us." (W.P.)

And Frank Conn wrote: "...it was all innocent fun in those days. If you got a cuddle and a kiss and maybe a date for the pictures you were very lucky."

While the care of parents for their children was the central core of family relationships, this support was often extended to include illegitimate children, siblings and elderly parents.

"...we classed them as our brothers because we didn't know. And they didn't know, not till years and years afterwards, cos mum brought them up as her own children. They didn't know – they knew they wasn't mum's children but they didn't know that the aunt was their mother. It was only that one day mum got out of temper and she said, I've had enough of you, you'll go back to your mother. I've had enough. My mother? he said, Who is my mother? So she said, Your aunt Alice. He said, I'll never speak to her as long as I live – and he never. He said, She's my mother and she's been coming in here all them years, and I didn't know. Course, he was upset, but he never spoke to her, after that." (Island woman)

"My earliest recollections of my Mother was the way she not only looked after my Father, sister and myself but also her siblings. My mother's three eldest brothers worked in the docks and each day they came to Mum for the midday meal. Wonderful meat puddings, stews, spotted dick, bread pudding and of course superb custard, needless to say none of it came out of a packet." (Kit Bragger, nee Bruce)

Before she married in 1931 Emma Cope found herself looking after her ailing mother and her future husband, his three brothers and their dad: "My life was completely taken up keeping my mother's home and theirs".

This was not universal, because Alf French recalled: "...an enormous number of these old people on their own", who he described as "spinsters, don't remember many bachelors, but certainly spinsters" and also elderly couples who had moved out of the family home to make room for the growing families of the next generation; he also cited "in-law problems" as making sharing a house "quite unworkable".

Childhood recollections include images of grandparents, relics of an earlier age, such as this from Ernest Bowler: "Grandma had asthma and smoked Potter's Asthma Herbs in a clay pipe. Grandad smoked evil-smelling tobacco. He had been a sailor, sailing before the mast, always seen in his "cheese-cutter" cap, arms like knotted rope."

These older people had been born and raised in Victorian times and had learnt to dread the penury of old age and the misery of the Workhouse. State pensions, introduced before the First World War, were not available to everyone and workplace pensions or private savings were rare. Many people, after a lifetime of hard work and struggle against poverty, had to rely on a combination of family support and public assistance in their old age. Everyone lived as cheaply as possible and worked as long as they were able to earn a few pence.

When a visit from the doctor cost a precious sixpence, he was avoided if possble and there were many home remedies. Some cures were as painful as the illness, like the treatment for boils and carbuncles, which were very common: "placing the neck of a steam-heated bottle firmly over the sore spot to draw out the infection... applying a scalding hot poultice made of either bread or potatoes or a mixture of both (or) wads of lint fished from a pan of scalding hot water." Coughs, colds and chest infections were treated with mustard poultices, camphorated oil, wintergreen embrocation and goose grease. As Dick Waterhouse said: "Whether or not these remedies were effective is a matter of opinion. We believed in them and that was important."

Childhood illnesses, which could be fatal, such as measles, mumps, chicken pox, scarlet fever and diphtheria, could not be cured by home-made remedies and sick children were often removed to an isolation hospital, sometimes for weeks on end.

Mrs Sarah Anne Knowles, nee Baker, of 140 Manchester Road, b.1854, d. 1930.

Otherwise the most commonly-used local hospital was St.Andrews, in Bow. Many people tried to keep up payments with the Hospital Savings Association to cover the cost of a stay in hospital though maternity care had to be paid for separately.

Although only called in as a last resort, Island doctors were well-known and liked. Doctor Mallea was described as "quite a character", who used to enjoy a glass of whisky in "Mac's", the *Princess of Wales* pub in Manchester Road, after his surgery.

Dr Mallea retired and was replaced in the 1930s by Dr Blasker, who moved there from Charing Cross Hospital. Margaret Hamilton recorded of this doctor: "He was keen on sport, and especially boxing, which he taught to the boys at the Dockland Settlement. This made him popular, quite apart from his practice. Before the Welfare State, he treated people for what they could afford. He was a friend as well as a doctor, a dear and kindly man who gave up his time to the Island as well as its people."

Home-made entertainment was as common as home-made medicine and more fun. Gladys Humphrey recalled: "Dad had two brothers, and a sister, and his dad, they all lived round us. So on Christmas Day we had the family in the evening, and then Boxing night Uncle John had us all to his house. Uncle Fred's turn was New Year's Eve. Everyone had a piano and we all had to sing. Grandad's song was *I'm forever blowing bubbles*. We seemed to sing a lot."

In the inter-war years sing-songs round the piano were gradually being replaced by gramophone records and, after the BBC was set up in 1922, the wireless:

"My father and his friend, as soon as the wireless papers used to come out – *Practical Wireless*, or *Wireless News* – they had blue-prints in, and they used to knock their heads together and start building wireless sets. Our living room was one massive great mass of bits of wire and sawn up bits and little switches and bits of crystal and cats' whiskers and what not. My mother used to go round to her mother's and one night, after she had left him soldering and messing about for weeks as he used to and she came back and he said, "'Ere, come and listen to this." He put the head phones on her and she was absolutely enthralled, because she had never heard the wireless before. She was sitting there with the head phones on and I said "Mum, can I have a bit of bread and jam", and she forgot she had the head phones on, she came to get me the bread and jam and pulled the lot on the floor". (George Thurgar)

"In the early '30s Dad bought his first second-hand wireless. Vaudeville was very popular, and Dad and I enjoyed the relayed football matches, given by a Mr Alison, whilst a background voice referring to a diagram printed in *The Radio Times*, said play was in square one, two etc." (Charles Corroyer)

George Henry Wright (1902-1982) in the living room of 131 Westferry Road, before his marriage in 1926.

Mr James and Mrs Emma McCartney of 158 East Ferry Road, listening to their crystal set, made by their son James, about 1923.

5. Social Life on the Island

Between the wars the population of the Island remained stable at around 21,000, the figure it had reached in 1900. Some better-off people were moving away, and those moving onto the Island tended to be the less well off – the Island offered the prospect of cheap accommodation close to the source of a variety of casual labouring work in the docks and factories. Cole (1981) described the population as becoming "progressively poorer". By 1929, only one quarter of household heads were in skilled occupations, the remaining three quarters were semi-skilled or unskilled.

The two key pillars of Island life which sustained people under difficult circumstances were those of work and family, and these are discussed in separate chapters. Strong bonds of friendship were forged in the workplace and many people were part of extended family networks, so that individuals were linked either by blood or marriage to others who were also neighbours, school friends and fellow workers. A life lived close to similar customs and overlapping areas of interest, could be full and satisfying. This closeness did not prevent arguments and fights, it may even have encouraged them, but long-term disagreements were the exception rather than the rule. Mr Huish said of life in Johnson Street: "Despite all the drawbacks, the people of the district were a very friendly lot and one knew almost everybody for a great distance around... vandalism and robbery were almost unknown and the only offenders were the occasional drunks... sometimes a very vocal and physical argument would occur between families which once settled was quickly forgotten." On the other hand, it *was* possible for two people to fall out and not speak to each other for years, even whilst living in the same street.

Outside the family and the workplace, social bonds were formed in the schools, the streets, sport, local politics, all kinds of clubs, church and chapel, and communal events such as processions, street parties, annual outings and hop-picking.

When a head teacher from St.Edmund's Roman Catholic School retired in 1925 after 19 years, the LCC's District Inspector wrote a special report to mark the occasion. It noted that teachers coming to "this isolated quarter" faced many difficulties – the journey long and subject to bad weather, the children from poor homes where "a necessarily narrow outlook" made it hard to attain "even an average standard of education". This school, with its 270 children in Infants and Mixed Departments, had a particular handicap in being next to a large iron works (Cutler's) and, being constructed on three floors with two rooms on each floor, involved the teachers in "much physical and nervous wear and tear".

But the report spoke glowingly of the courageous and happy spirit of the staff and their strong sense of duty to and interest in the children. Their punctuality and loyalty were given special mention, also singled out was "the excellence of discipline and tone". The Report went on: "Although the boys of this district are vigorous and are regarded, even by men, as not easy to manage, there is no sign of disorder or insubordination, but on the contrary their behaviour is steady, their manners definitely good and their attitude to their elders in school pleasant."

As well as St.Edmund's School, there were two Church of England schools, St.Luke's and St.John's. The school originally run by Christ Church had become Cubitt Town School, in Wharf Road (later Saunders Ness Road). Much later, St.Luke's moved to that site. At the Manchester Road end of Glengall Road was Glengall Road Elementary School (later the site of Cubitt Town School); on the Millwall side of the Island were the Janet Street school for children with learning difficulties, the Isle of Dogs School, and Millwall Central School where clever children could stay until 16, learning languages and business skills. British Street School, founded by the School Board for London, was the original name of the modern Harbinger School.

From 1919 onwards, children had to stay at school until the age of 14. Many Island children were bright enough, but very few came from families sufficiently well off, to stay on after 14 at either the Central School, or one of the local Grammar Schools. Scholarships did not cover the full cost of further education, and more than one Islander has remembered with regret that: "Dad would not let me stay on", or "I knew my parents could not afford to keep me at school". The outbreak of war in 1939 prevented Bill O'Neil from taking up his place at George Green School in East India Dock Road, which, he says, was a pity, because: "My Dad had gone without a few pints and packets of fags to buy my uniform!"

This individual misfortune had a positive side, in that these children, who today would be going away to university, then remained in the community, becoming the intelligent, articulate adults who took leading roles in trade unions, in local politics and in public and community service of all kinds.

Basic elementary education could be a happy learning experience and a lot depended on the character and ability of the teachers, some of whom stayed for years at the same school.

"We lived in Lead Street near the Fire Station. I went to British Street School (later Harbinger) when I was three years old. The first year, in the "Babies" class, I remember the sand pit and a large dolls' house, also the lovely big coal fire in the corner, it had

Glengall Road School in 1935-36. Back row, third from left, David Mulford; sixth from left, Rose Marsh (later Wood); last on right, Maud Taylor; second row, second from left, Christine Hearson; third, Doreen Sapsford.

a large guard around it. We all had to have a sleep on little beds, or was it mats on the floor. I went to all the classes in the Infants to the top class, and then up to the first floor to what we called "the big girls".

In the last two classes before I left school two new teachers came, a Miss Bedding and Miss Boroughs, they were young, and made us feel grown up. One day George Bernard Shaw came to our school, shook hands with some of the pupils, and made a speech in the hall.

We went on a school journey to Devon in the summer when I was 12 years old. We stayed at the Pendragon Hotel. Miss Bedding came with us, she came to our room one night and told us about "the birds and the bees" (we already knew). We went to the beach and went diving in the surf, we had a lovely time.

In that year the school had the new name of Harbinger and we had to have a uniform to go away with the school, it was burgundy and blue, West Ham colours."

St.Luke's School, which was in Westferry Road, is remembered as being: "a tall brick building, L-shaped, with a steeply gabled roof." Next door to the school in the 1930s was a bottle factory and one pupil remembered: "the clinking and clashing sound of glass; this was practically incessant...the workers seemed to be forever dumping down, picking up and generally moving around, crates of bottles".

"Empire Day was the highlight of our calendar. We would march to the Parish Hall in Havannah Street and sit cross-legged on the floor. On the stage would be the Headmaster and Headmistress and various dignitaries. Patriotic speeches were orated, interspersed with songs like *Jerusalem* and *Land of Hope and Glory*. The famous speech from Shakespeare, beginning "This royal throne of kings, this sceptred Isle" would be delivered. After this came the part we had all been looking forward to: as we filed out, each child would be handed an orange and a marzipan fish. Then we had the rest of the day off."

Another highlight of the year in some schools was the May Day celebration, with dancing round the Maypole and the crowning of a Queen.

Home circumstances made studying difficult:

"When I was doing homework, I had to wait until the table was cleared and somebody else would possibly be wanting to use the table, everything was done on there, but by arrangement I could have half an hour to do my homework, or sometimes I'd do it in the bedroom but the bedroom was a difficult place to do things in because bedrooms were shared and you had other people coming in and going out...you had to prop your books up on the bed....The good thing in those days was that the libraries did allow children to go in and do their homework. We had to walk over to Strattondale Street, to the library there. They had a sort of children's reference room, where there were tables. You could combine it with changing your books, if you belonged to the library.

My own mother and father, they never came to school, unless something happened and their attention was necessary. They weren't alone in this. This was general...parents were very much concerned with the business of keeping a home and earning a living and so life was a bit austere, and it was not a common thing to find the sort of bond of affection between parents and children in the 1920s that one finds today. What the children did at school – the parents – it didn't occur to them to become involved because they were involved in so many other things."

The games the children played in the playground and in the streets were left behind when they moved into the adult world of work at 14. The Good Friday tradition of skipping in the street was the exception. Large ropes begged or borrowed from the nearest rope works were stretched across the streets and grown women turned the ropes and took turns to skip as they had done when little girls. Several people remembered this custom, whose origins are unknown. It died away, like many street games, with the Second World War and the coming of motor traffic.

Street games of football and cricket were part of childhood as well as preparation for the adult world. Football in particular was extraordinarily popular on the Island. All the schools had teams and teachers encouraged the sport.

Recording his memories of Glengall Road School, William Chapman wrote: "As different teachers came back healed from their war wounds, our lives were moulded from their different dedications and abilities. The first one back was a sports master, Mr Simmons, who was extremely popular, especially with the older boys who had known him previously before he had joined up. There had been a very good football team until then but it had been dropped when he left. He soon set about finding the nucleus of another team to compete with every school in the East End and Tower Hamlet Division. A woman teacher came to our rescue and fitted us all out with football gear – jerseys, boots, shorts, corner flags, the whole lot. The excitement was great, especially as some of the boys had never had a pair of boots that fitted them in their lives. A league was formed and you never saw such a keen and dedicated bunch of kids in your life.

We travelled every Saturday morning by train to Victoria Park to a numbered pitch. We gradually became one of the top teams of the East End Schools. The two teams we could not beat were the boys from Shenfield, an orphanage where they showed us how football should be played, and the other being Millwall Central, where a few boys from our school went if they passed the scholarship exam. We were bitter rivals, being in the same road and with them being so superior."

Every pub, workplace, church, chapel or neighbourhood had its team or group of teams. Enthusiasm was fired by the successes of local boys like "Banger" Bill Voisey who became England team manager and later Millwall Manager. Local pitches included the land opposite the Lead Works in Westferry Road, parts of the Mudchute and the "New Park" and any spare space in factory yard or around the dock area would do to kick a ball around during a break in the working day. Island teams were often successful in local competition. Alf Cottage recalled of one Dockland Settlement team: "Out of two thousand teams, we reached the final of the London Junior Cup, levelled in the Kent League, and won the Dockland Cup a few times." Nationally, football was big business. The fortunes of favourite professional teams, notably West Ham and Millwall, were followed passionately through the newspapers and by attendance at matches whenever possible.

Boxing was another great Island sport. There were several clubs for boys, and a few made it to professional status. William Chapman wrote: "Boxing at the Dockland Settlement was three nights a week. Our instructor was an ex-professional named Tom Cherry, but he had lost his agility and when he put the gloves on with some of the lads they knocked hell out of him so after a while he just gave us advice from outside the ring.

One of our main attractions was a small building in the yard of a big pub, the *Dock House*. There was just enough room for a boxing ring and one row of chairs each side. All the local lads used to fight there once or twice a week of an evening when they reached the professional ranks. There were no other training facilities around. Quite a few names spring to mind – Wag Bennett, Ernie Jarvis, the Softleys. We used to get on the roof and hang over the skylight." Palmer also emphasises the popularity of boxing: "A Poplar lad, Teddy Baldock, became Bantamweight Champion of the World in May 1927 when he defeated Archie Bell at the Albert Hall. A fleet of 52 hired buses brought his fans from Poplar to Kensington Gore for the fight."

Top picture opposite:
Wesleyan Athletic Club Cricket Team, includes G. Polding, Walter Williams, Fred Williams, Arthur Williams, Griffiths Noal and Lou Mace. 1920s.

Lower Picture:
St.Cuthbert's House Football Club, 1927-28.
Back row: C. Williams, R. Miller, W. Finch, R. Templeman, P. Caygill, M. Collins.
Middle: G. Ray, C. Codgell (trainer), H. Black, W. Whyberd, W. Moyse (HonSec.)
Front: J. Porter, W. Jenkins, S. Saville (Capt.), W. Lock, F. Avis.
Foreground: J. Spence and D. Jones.

Boxer Wag Bennett, of Millwall, in the 1920s.

"Tammy Jarvis went to America and won his fight and when he came home he was wearing a ten gallon Stetson hat, in white, with a white suit and shoes. He had a broom handle of a cigar!" recalled Mrs L. Chapman. Tammy bought a greengrocer's shop in Westferry Road with his earnings.

Girls and young women had even fainter prospects of getting into the glamorous world of professional success and big money, though they dreamed of stardom in films or on the stage.

Jean Whitton (nee Taphouse) was introduced to the "theatrical world" by a Mrs Rogers who lived opposite Maconochies in West Ferry Road and who started a singing and dancing class, two nights a week in her own front room. Jean says: " ...after a number of rehearsals we would perform in the hall of St. Cuthbert's. Our costumes were made of any odd scraps of material and old net curtains, transformed for one of the numbers, *A Gay Little Girl from Japan*, into a geisha style. My dear Mum and I made the costumes. On one occasion we put on a show in the Dockland Settlement where we performed *The Sheik of Araby*."

Cycling and dancing came to prominence in this period. The Island had several cycling clubs, tandems

A member of the Dolly Dell dance troupe, 1930s.

ushered into the gym for refreshments. There we were seated at long tables, while members of the mothers' club, dressed as serving maids, waited on us..."

The mass media was just beginning to make its mark through the cinema and radio, but the tradition of self-made entertainment was alive and full of vigour on the Island, where talented Islanders were forming their own bands, concert troupes and drama groups. A concert given by Arthur Crane and his Black Dominoes Orchestra at the Dockland Settlement in 1928 included among the performers Miss Alice Lloyd (actually Mrs Arthur Crane), soprano, Arthur Crane on his violin, Harry Anderson on his Ukelele, and George Morris on the piano, all Islanders. Arthur Crane, whose family ran a newsagents shop in Westferry Road, left the Island in 1941 and moved to Surrey. He made a career out of music, ending by leading the Guildford Light Orchestra for 21 years and was still playing the violin at the age of 89.

The Dockland Settlement charity had been founded by Sir Reginald Kennedy Cox. During World War One he recruited a young officer, Captain Kimberley (Kim), to become a resident assistant at the Canning Town Settlement. When Kim learned that the Welcome Institute on the Island was to close, as its warden was retiring, he persuaded Kennedy-Cox to buy the building. This was done and the new club, Dockland Settlement No.2, was opened in September 1923, with Kim as resident warden. Kim persuaded his influential friends to give time, money and materials to help in launching and equipping the Settlement and their support continued for many years. As life-long member Alf Cottage put it:

"Kim seemed to know all the Lords and Ladies and Royal Family. I went in the Royal Box at the Albert Hall to see *Hiawatha* with Charles Laughton and company, and also visited Lord Luard's estate.

were popular, and young people made long journeys away from the Island

"...pre-war we was great cycling enthusiasts. We bought a tandem, my brother bought a tandem, we was all courting, we went everywhere, you know, cycle to work, cycle in the evening, over to Eltham for a cup of tea and cycle back. This is the way life was."(Bernie Bannister) For those who had no bicycles, hiking was an alternative – through the foot-tunnel and over Blackheath into the Kent countryside on a Saturday afternoon.

Dancing, in the era which saw the arrival of the gramophone, the radio, jazz, and the big band, was a great joy. "I used to go dancing every night, yes, even Sunday night, at the Dockland Settlement, the Masonic Hall in Greenwich, and St. Edmund's church hall."

George Hames wrote: "At the Dockland Settlement, every Saturday night was given over to dancing, with occasional costume balls, such as the Costers' Ball, and the Tramps' Ball. But nothing equalled the Tudor Ball, held to celebrate the Silver Jubilee of King George and Queen Mary in 1935. Nearly 300 guests, all in Tudor costume, danced to the music of Arthur Crane's "Black Dominoes", who were dressed in green tunics with white ruffles in a minstrels gallery built on the stage. The dance lasted until 3 in the morning. At midnight we were all

Violet Brunt (later McCarthy), Babs Peacock, Helen Hames, Renee Hames and George Hames, dressed for the Tudor Ball at the Dockland Settlement, 1935.

Helen Wates, Elizabeth Suter, Susan Allen and Joan Dewey, who ran St.Mildred's Settlement in the 1920s and 1930s.

The first summer holiday camp was at Lord Beaulieu's estate at Southampton; another holiday was on the Norfolk Broads at Stalham on another large estate."

The Settlement eventually became a family club, enjoyed by generations of Islanders. Activities included gymnastics, table-tennis, boxing, swimming, soccer, cricket, athletics, netball, dress-making, handicrafts, badminton, choral singing and dramatics.

Drama at the Dockland Settlement included "...the annual Federation Shakespeare for boys only (and)we used to write and produce our own shows, varieties and excerpts from productions like *Showboat* and *The Student Prince* and *White Horse Inn*. We did a nativity play at Christmas, *The Upper Room* at Easter. Our greatest success was the full cast production of *The Merchant of Venice*."

St.Mildred's Settlement had been founded, with the support of the Anglican church, in 1897 and was run by women from middle-class families who "settled" on the Island where they helped to run a programme of social activities and welfare work. In 1925 St.Mildred's offered girls and young women a choice of Guides and Brownies, club nights with singing, dancing, games, drama and Bible study as well as camping holidays and visits to the country houses of the wealthy friends of the residents.

In the 1930s the House was "full of clubs" and every August 400 children went to cottages all over England under the Children's Country Holiday Fund, to which parents also contributed. Factory girls and mothers went on seaside holidays and the Senior Club and Rangers went to Belgium and Switzerland respectively in 1938.

Membership of any of the Island's churches and chapels provided a social life for those who had the time and energy to enjoy it – mainly the younger generation.

One Islander recalled:"As a family my brother Norman and sister Stella (who sadly died aged six) and my parents, of course, were very involved with the Methodist Chapel in Manchester Road. For many years my father was organist there and we children were expected to attend Sunday School and other activities. Edith Fothergill and Dan Hubbard led the Sunday School. the Hubbard family worked very hard for us. Mrs Hubbard and her daughter Greta organised an annual play. We did *Dick Whittington* one year and every child had a part. They had infinite patience.

During the week there were other activities such as the Christian Endeavour Group and the Girls' Life Brigade. The latter was run by Miss Marjorie Knightsbridge, whose father had a butcher's shop in Chrisp street. He was also a lay preacher. I attended two camps with the GLB, one at the Isle of Sheppey and the other near Herne Bay."

The Methodist Chapel in Alpha Grove had a congregation of 150 adults and a Sunday School of

Father Kingdon, vicar of St.John's Church, Cubitt Town, for many years.

9th South Poplar Scouts in camp at Ockley, Surrey, in the 1920s. Amongst them: Mariner, Rangecroft, Humphries and Smith. Scoutmaster G.Hill, Cubmaster, R.Taylor.

Bridget and Patrick O'Neill, in front of their home at 202 Westferry Road, a terrace between The Ironmongers and the Magnet and Dewdrop. The altar was built for Corpus Christi, a festival in June. In the upper window is a smaller altar built by Nellie Devlin.

300 children in 1926 and Alpha Hall was built to accommodate them. The famous Rev.W.H.Lax, of Poplar, helped to raise the funds. There was a branch of "Toc H" meeting in St.Luke's Hall, famous for their sing-songs accompanied on the American organ by Ed Ellis.

And for Bernie Bannister: "A lot of our life, my life, was wrapped around the church, St.Edmund's, because we had a wonderful scout troop down there...terrific scout troop we had. You had a social life down at the church and we used to go to Arundel in the back of a lorry, for a dollar, for a fortnight, all the scouts. Terrific troop they was, Bill Budd was the scout master and Sid Howard was assistant master, and all that crowd. I know of nine who were killed during the war. My brother Bill was in the cubs, Vic was in the scouts, we was all wrapped up in scouts all the time...So you alternated your social life and your dock life, I was friends with the sons, the dads I worked with in the dock.... "

There were several scout groups on the Island, most of them attached to one of the churches. The leader at St.Luke's was the much-loved Rowland Dowlen, who was captured and executed as a spy during the war. At St.Paul's Presbyterian Church (now The Space) the 9th South Poplar Troop enjoyed boxing, football, camping and hiking and took part in team competitions with other troops, visited other groups and went on outings to museums and shows.

The Island's churches and chapels all offered their members opportunities for social interaction and entertainment, as well as spiritual comfort. The religious census of 1903 had revealed that only just over 11% of the Island's population actually attended church or chapel regularly, and half of these were children. Attendances dwindled up to 1939 (due to the decline of the middle-class population and the growing popularity of other forms of Sunday pastime) and it is clear that regular church- and chapel-goers were in a minority. However a substantially larger number used their local place of worship for weddings, christenings and funerals.

One religious occasion which, according to memory, drew in all sections of the population, was the annual Catholic procession and dressing of windows.

More from Bernie Bannister: "Eileen's brother Arthur he was our troop leader and we used to walk in processions and of course that was a great day on the Island. If you were Catholics or non-Catholics, the outdoor procession was the day. We lived in the first banjo in the Crescent and we always had an altar, a grotto they call them now. My father got drunk, then the priest would come round in the evening and bless the altar. It was a good social day...wonderful atmosphere... we used to have Sunday evening benediction then go dancing, didn't we, a tanner, social dancing, piano and drums, a great life, all denominations, it didn't matter, everybody came along, in St.Edmund's School."

Arthur Smith, born 1912, the youngest son of Mr and Mrs G.B.Smith, of 13 Ship Street. A choirboy at Christ Church, he was also a keen footballer and played for Millwall Youth. When he left school he worked for steel stockholders Cargo Fleet, in Saunders Ness Road.

To make the "altar", the whole window casement would be removed and a tiered stand erected in the window. White sheets were draped over the structure and the religious ornaments, pictures and candles were displayed alongside a vase of lilies. Underneath each altar, says one memory: "...was a crate or barrel of beer, if not both".

A more solemn occasion, which also united all Islanders, was Remembrance Day, which, Dennis Dawson recalled: "...in those days was strictly observed by everyone. At 11am on the 11th of November everything and every person, including all traffic, came to a standstill for the two minutes silence and there truly was a silence everywhere... the First World War with its tremendous number of casualties was vividly in everyone's thoughts, as it was still comparatively recent."

Islanders who had the time, money and inclination for pastimes outside the home and workplace

An outing from The Vulcan in Westferry Road, includes Bill Harman, Bill Sales, Sid Thompson, George Field, Albert Avis senior and Albert Avis junior, Tim Marshall, George Locke junior, George Locke senior, Bill Conway junior and Bill Conway senior.

had a range of options, starting, unless they were teetotal, with the public house. Apart from a much-needed drink after a working all day in hot, dirty, dusty conditions, pubs offered the opportunity to socialise with work-mates and peers. Women never went into pubs on their own. This would have been considered "very, very fast". A few older women might, sometimes, on a weekday or a Sunday morning, go with three or four cronies and sit in the snug, having a glass of stout and shelling their peas or some similar task. If married couples went to the pub together it was usually on a Friday or Saturday night with friends and neighbours, or on special occasions such as a family wedding, birthday or a funeral.

Class distinctions survived. In the 1920s, the *Newcastle Arms (later the Waterman's Arms)* still had a bar which was exclusive to "craftsmen" such as shipwrights. Stokers and those in similar occupations would go into another bar. However, this separation between skilled and unskilled was beginning to fade out. The main distinction was in the furnishings and appearance of the two bars. The floor of the public bar was strewn with sawdust, this was to absorb any spittle which failed to reach the spittoons standing at strategic intervals. The furnishings were plain wooden benches. The saloon bar, by contrast, had wood-panelled walls and a carpeted floor. A small separate section was the "jug and bottle", the off-licence where anyone, including young children doing errands for adults, could be served.

Pubs were the headquarters of many local clubs, with a predominantly male membership, as the list put together by Cole would suggest. He found: "...Freemasons, Oddfellows, Foresters, Buffaloes, Millwall and Cubitt Town Horticultural Society, the Allotment Society, the Poplar Municipal Gardening Guild, the Millwall Esperanto Society, the Millwall Fellowship Club for the Unemployed, the Millwall Poultry Club, the Poplar, Blackwall and District Rowing Club, a theatrical society, a bowls association, several Millwall Lion fan clubs and countless pigeon racing and rabbit groups."

Island men kept chickens and caged birds as well as pigeons and rabbits. These hobbies, which were nation-wide, formed entire sub-cultures with their specialist magazines, local, regional and national shows and exhibitions.

The North Greenwich Bowls Club was founded in 1901, when it was also a founder member of the London Parks Bowling Association. It was originally the exclusive domain of ratepayers, particularly local shop-keepers, who, according to Huish: "...had a very close affinity which amounted almost to a brotherhood. One could be sure that come Thursday, early closing day, many could be found in Island Gardens playing bowls on what was a superb bowling green." The general public were admitted after World War One. The early 1920s were golden years for the club. One member, Mr W.F.Beattie, was President of the London Parks Bowling Association in 1921 and in 1922 the club won the London Parks Trophy. Also in 1922, NGBC boasted an international player, Mr W.T.Bishop, who played for England.

Like religion, politics was a minority interest amongst Islanders. Cole's research into Island life in the years between the wars led him to the conclusion that: "Poplar went Labour post-war and was noted for its radicalism, but this applied more to Bow and north Poplar than to the Island, which was relatively quiescent". Palmer (2000) notes that Labour's striking gains in the 1919 London County Council elections resulted in social reformers dominating the borough councils in Hackney, Bethnal Green and

An outing from The Ship in Westferry Road in the 1920s. Top row, in the coach: Arthur Justice (worked at rope works) and Bill Audit (also a rope maker); standing, Fred Oliver, (rope maker); Nat Oliver (worked at oil mill); Wally Green; Harry McSweeney (stevedore); Rueben and Jack Oliver (both worked at McDougall's). Centre front, Fred Payne, landlord, and looking out of window, baby Lily Payne.

North Greenwich Bowls Club in 1922. The shield on the left is the Buxton Shield, donated by Sir Sydney Buxton, M.P., the club's perpetual trophy, awarded annually to the reigning champion, with a smaller shield added each year. The circular shield in the centre is the London Parks' Trophy, won by North Greenwich Bowls Club in 1922.

Poplar. They were also virtually in control of the Poor Law Boards, responsible for the welfare of the old, the sick, the poor and the unemployed. Famously, Poplar Councillors were imprisoned in 1921 for flouting government rules about the level of rates and the amounts to be spent on poor relief. Their six weeks' imprisonment led to new laws, equalising the rates, and "for several years Poplar and other Boroughs on both sides of the Lea continued to spend money on relief far above the Government limits." (Palmer) Labour continued to hold Poplar and other East London Boroughs for many years. The imprisoned Councillors were re-elected again and again. "Sam March sat for South Poplar from 1922 until 1931, when on his death he was succeeded in the seat by another imprisoned colleague, David Adams."

Labour Councillors presided over what Palmer describes as "the most revolutionary social change for East Enders between the wars", that was, the provision of council housing for rent. They also introduced a range of measures to improve health and welfare. The Island's isolation, poverty and high proportion of unskilled labourers made union organisation relatively weak (except amongst the port workers and some skilled trades such as the engineers), and the fact that Labour did not have to campaign hard to get elected meant there was relatively little debate or education around political issues. However, life stories reveal that individual Islanders were more interested in politics than Cole's dismissive "quiescent" would suggest.

During the nine-day General Strike of May 1926, the workers, through local Councils of Action, tried to control transport and communications in their own areas, making and implementing their own decisions about what work was essential, and putting out Strike Bulletins to keep the public informed. The roads leading to and from the docks became a focus of confrontation as troops were brought in to enforce the movement of goods in and out of the docks. The memories of Islanders who witnessed these events suggest that the experience nurtured a long-lasting radicalism:

Mr Charlton: "...we all marched from the Poplar Town Hall that used to be in Newby Place, we all marched outside to have a meeting. And when we got there, they never even give them time to put their stands up to make a speech. The police and that came out with their horses and mowed us down and started using truncheons and everything else and that was in 1926 and then old Churchill said "Fetch the army out and shoot them down". That's true as I'm here, yes, fetch the horses in the public houses in the top of Blackwall Tunnel there, at *The Volunteer*, in that pub there, fetch the horses in to chuck the people out and half of them people marching all the way to – and never got a chance. They were trying to make a speech but they were knocked down, they didn't have an earthly chance...."

Mr Green: "Yes, we was all on strike, everybody. We got nothing, did we. We never got no satisfaction, but what I mean to say is this, the unions were born on that day. They brought the General Transport Workers in... that was a good enough union to pay everybody that joined ten bob a week strike pay, and they went broke over it. But they built themselves up then, did the Transport and General."

George Thurgar recalled: "My uncle Tom was quite interested in Communism. He was quite a bit of a radical to my Dad, although my Dad was staunch Labour. In fact I can't remember any Conservatives

John Francis Gilbertson, Mayor of Poplar 1938-39. He was a dry dock worker and lived in Havannah Street. He was on the executive of his union for 18 years, was treasurer of the local Labour Party, and represented Cubitt Town as a Labour Councillor from 1933.

around that way. They couldn't afford to be. There might have been some amongst the elite of the area...they lived in ordinary houses but they seemed a bit more affluent than anyone else."

Harry Sparks had been a Labour Party activist all his life. He came from a family which was "well off by Island standards" but "I knew there were kids in my classes at school who lived on bread and marge from Monday through Saturday, when Mum boiled up a few butcher's scraps to make Sunday's thanksgiving less of a mockery."

George Chamberlain, of Seyssel Street, was remembered by his daughter Hilda as having been: "a school manager, a Poplar Borough councillor and secretary of the local branch of the General and Municipal Workers' Union... also a very keen member of and worker for the Labour Party."

For most Islanders, most of the time, Island life provided all they needed – home, work, family and whatever social life they had the resources for. Trips away were rare, though the 1930s saw more opportunities in this respect as cycling became more popular and roads improved to accommodate the motor vehicle.

Mr Huish wrote that: '...the roads were being improved and the new dual carriageway to Southend was opened with accompanying cycle tracks. The nearest seaside resorts to East London were beginning

An outing from The London pub, Cubitt Town, in 1938. Includes Mrs Spenton, Mrs Bradford (the landlady), Mrs Hullett, Mrs Nicholls, Ray Hammond, Anna Weston, Liz Northeast, Marie Hardy, Alma Hardy and Jean Nicholls.

to enjoy a really busy period. Southend, Margate, Ramsgate and Clacton became quite easy to reach for a day's enjoyment. Train travel also was becoming cheaper and more comfortable..."

Outings to Southend by pleasure steamer were a popular treat for families and groups. There were quite a few of these, the Belle boats, *Laguna, Southend, Yarmouth*, and *London Belle, as well as* the General Steam Navigation boats, *The Golden Eagle* and *Crested Eagle*.

The annual outing or "beano" from workplace or local pub were traditionally occasions for letting the hair down. Sometimes these were provided at the company's expense, and pub outings were normally saved for during the year. Crates of beer on the coach, and frequent stops for more refreshment on the way home, were normal procedure on these occasions, especially for the all-male outings. Some companies laid on an annual dinner-dance at a central London venue, though these were usually for office workers

and directors only. The entire workforce of Pinchin and Johnson's Paint Works in Wharf Road went by motor charabanc to Wembley Stadium for the Exhibition in 1925.

In the inter-war years the cinema largely replaced the music hall as the most popular form of mass entertainment. According to Palmer there were over 50 cinemas in the East End by 1935. The Island had a makeshift cinema (using a white painted wall as a screen) for only a brief period, and Islanders trekked to either Poplar or Greenwich for their films.

"Every Saturday morning hordes of children were seen making their way to the nearest cinemas, whatever the weather. The "Blue Lights" in Greenwich was ours, which meant going through the foot tunnel and only three minutes away was this wonderful, magical world of make-believe. There was a short newsreel, the main feature film, thrilling serials, a good two-and-a-half hours of excitement and suspense. Then we descended on the outside world and raced home through the Tunnel, chasing and charging each other, acting like the heroes and heroines we'd just left behind..

These same cinemas were well patronised by adults and every evening queues of people patiently waited for the doors to open. While queuing we were entertained by the street buskers performing as jugglers, accordion players, tap dancers and singers."

During the 1930s, trade unions campaigned successfully for more workers to have holidays with pay, but on the Island it was still exceptional for a family to go away and stay in a boarding house at the seaside. St.Mildred's ran schemes to send hard-worked mothers and poor children away for a change of scene, but otherwise the closest most people came to a holiday was an annual visit to the Kentish hop-fields. This was a tradition in many families. Hopping was organised by women; they hired lorries or caught a train; they took with them their dependent children and some basic equipment – bedding and cooking utensils. Dick Waterhouse recalled:

"Who could forget the moment of arrival at first light on a warm misty morning (having left New Cross station at midnight), being lifted up on to the big farm wagon which had come to pick us up and take us to the farm. Having got the key to the shed which was to be our home for the duration, Mother got a fire going and had a brew-up for breakfast. My memories of that early morning tea are everlasting. The fragrant aroma of tea brewed in an open pan outdoors over a wood fire is something to savour for ever, because no tea brewed indoors ever tasted or smelt the same to me."

The hop-pickers slept in wooden huts on straw-filled sacks, cooked over open fires, and worked all day, while the children helped or minded each other. At weekends, other family members visited, roast dinners were contrived and business boomed in the local pubs. After five or six weeks, they all came back

Cooking over the open fire during hop-picking at Leeds Abbey, Maidstone, Kent, in the 1930s. On the right, Mrs Lillian Kilgour, of Poplar.

to the Island, laden with "hopping apples" and the money they'd earned.

Islanders had many aspects of social life in common, but there were divisions within the community. These were based on status and behaviour, as well as on the geographical boundaries which separated one neighbourhood from another. Distinctions were made on the grounds of trade union membership, such as the "blues" and "whites" of the dock workers; on the grounds of religion – the Protestants and Catholics; on the grounds of employment – skilled and unskilled, white-collar and blue-collar; on the grounds of morality, encompassing such character traits as neighbourliness, honesty within certain limits, and cleanliness, the outward sign of a virtuous life. Cole points out that people can only be assessed on their character in this way in a settled community, where family background and personal circumstances are known.

James Mee's recollections reveal some of the finer distinctions which were made between one street and another:

"That side of the Island like Manchester Road and places like Pier Street, they all tended to be, or they thought they were, a little bit better than the part round where I used to live (British Street) as it was all industrial. I think the houses were better there too, they seemed to be a better class of house. You know Mellish Street? Well, that was always called "piano, pride and poverty street" because they were quite nice-looking houses but people always said, Well, you know, they've got pianos but they've got no grub, how people used to talk then. Stewart Street, The Bay as we used to call it, a terrible name that had, every other family either had somebody in prison or just come out. there again, they couldn't all have been bad, but us kids used to say, You keep away from The Bay, don't you go round there. What they thought would happen I don't know. I suppose us kids magnified it too. The row of houses I thought of as being the cat's whiskers was Charteris Terrace along East Ferry Road there, 50 years ago they were fairly new and they were the first ones that had baths in them".

Other anecdotal evidence confirmed the reputation of Stewart Street: "...more fights and arguments round the Bay, so many more kiddies, bigger families... you know, hell of a lot of people round there, that caused more problems, husbands was always on the booze and the fights Saturday night was nobody's business, oh, it used to be a pantomime!" And of Charteris Terrace it was said that: "The kids didn't play out like the other kids. You would only see them walking past with their mothers."

And there were divisions even within Mellish

Street, remembered by William Chapman:

"I realise I am privileged to have been born and dragged up, as we termed it, amongst such wonderful people. They had their faults and some wrong'uns, the same as anywhere else, but to me the only fault that sticks out is the one of "snobbery". I believe it was due to the economic and social struggles of the times. Mellish Street, being of a superior type of houses, was occupied by superior people. There was one section of the street of a poorer type, known as "the blocks", being constructed of four flats with a centre stairway from the street up to the first floor flats and from the rear down to a large yard. We moved there in 1918.

When the Great War ended we had a Peace Party in the street for us children. But us children being from the blocks were barred from sitting with the kids from the better houses. We were invited to sit at separate tables in a further section of the street, although in ratio there were more men from the blocks in the armed forces than in the rest of the street."

There was another street party in Mellish Street to celebrate the coronation in 1937, organised by the residents. Eight door-to-door collectors (residents Messrs Bines, Chapman, Cowling, Gilbertson, Platt, Marsden, Smeede and Smith) raised nearly eighty pounds from people living in the street and there were additional donations by local factory owners and shopkeepers of just under four pounds. The money was spent on 200 teas at one shilling and threepence, great quantities of flags, bunting, streamers, plaques, ice cream, fruit, hats, small prizes, printing, the hire of conjurer, clown and piano, and a telegram to the King and Queen for four shillings and sixpence. Three pounds was distributed to local children at threepence per head and the balance of three shillings and twopence sent to Shadwell Children's Hospital. Every item was accounted for in the printed balance sheet.

During the Second World War the Island population, whatever its internal divisions, was to be united in fear and defiance. As a result of the war Islanders were to be scattered and regrouped in new communities with the addition of incomers from other parts of London.

Old social patterns were to disappear whilst new pastimes and new forms of entertainment would take their place in the post-war world. But the strong sense of neighbourliness and of place, which characterised the Island during the inter-war years, would show itself again in the 1950s and 1960s as Islanders faced the challenge of recovery and reconstruction.

Street party in Plevna Street, Cubitt Town, probably the 1935 Jubilee of King George V.

6. The Second World War

A European war was expected in 1938, the time of the "Munich crisis" but Prime Minister Chamberlain returned triumphantly to London from Germany with Hitler's offer of "peace in our time". This was, however, short-lived.

During this crisis, in a rehearsal for what was to come, the ladies of St. Mildred's Settlement recorded that: "gas masks were issued and plans made for evacuation... trenches were dug in the football ground opposite the Lead Works...the docks sprouted guns in many and strange places and Warwickshire mingled with Cockney, Millwall Fellowship club premises were handed over to anti-aircraft units for a recreation room..." And Bill O'Neill remembered: "strange-looking vehicles appearing, fire engines painted green, rescue service vehicles, ARP posts being set up, street air raid shelters being built."

According to Bill, the evacuation plans which the government had prepared were actually put in hand at this time:

"I was put down for evacuation. I had my case packed, my labels on and even got as far as assembling at St.Edmund's School and if I remember rightly the buses were there waiting, when news came through of Mr Chamberlain's visit to Munich. We all went home and those that had got away came back, a lot of children from Millwall had gone to the Abingdon and Somerset areas and from what we heard we didn't think we had missed much. There was no large river, no streets to play in and it was very dark at night!"

Within less than a year, war was again imminent and Bernard Bannister was one of many young men called up from the docks:

"A lot of them, by the time war broke out they were in their forties and forty-fives, some were too old for calling up, I mean I have worked with men who were in their seventies, dockers on the quay, pulling the trucks around at seventy...but there wasn't so many young men in the docks, because you had to be twenty-one anyway before you got in. So the maximum of young men were about 30...and those...had either gone already or were on the point of joining up. I have never known one bloke who was a conscientious objector. No, no way. You had a job to do and that was the end of it...this is for your King and country and you accepted it as part of your job and you just went and that was it."

Sidney Marsh and his daughter Rose, of Stewart Street, outside the miner's home in County Durham where Rose and her brothers were evacuated. Mr Marsh had made friends with sailors who were from mining families, through his job at the London Graving Dock, and when war broke out one of them invited the children to stay with them.

On 1st September 1939, Island children assembled at their schools to board coaches on the first stage of their journey into the unknown. Each child bore a label on which their name and the name of their school was written. Many teachers accompanied the children on their journeys so that schools could stay together during evacuation. Miss Laid was Head of the Infants' Department of the Isle of Dogs School in 1935. When war came she and another teacher, Miss Lucas, took 400 children to Wells in Somerset and she stayed with them till in 1942 she came back as Head of the Infants' in Glengall School. She retired from her post as Head of Cubitt Town School in 1954.

Although pregnant mothers, and those with children under school age, qualified for official

Tobruk, 1942. Centre, Arthur French, of Chapel House Street, who won the George medal for taking a barge laden with ammunition safely out to sea. On the right, Bernard Bannister, of Hesperus Cresent, who later married Arthur's sister Eileen.

evacuation, most parents were left behind. Naturally, it was heart-rending:

"The war broke out about thirty-nine, didn't it? Cos my children was only young – they all went away. I can remember it well, I shall never forget it, I was choked seeing 'em go, you know. We all see 'em outside the school in the buses and all waving goodbye...all tears running down your face...it was 'ard, you know, cos you think to yourself, they're going and you never know if you'll see 'em again, but thank God...".

Mrs Grace Skinner had a large family born before the Second World War. When war came, her older children went into various branches of the armed forces and her younger children were evacuated, so she was suddenly very much alone: "Alan was only five when he went down there...it broke my heart....I got that way, I suppose it played on my mind, I used to stand at the gate waiting for them to come home for their dinner knowing they wasn't coming home, people used to say, Grace, your children are not coming home. Anyway, I got over that...".

Catherine Newberry's mother described the situation to her as: "...awful, so quiet and eerie. There was no sound of little voices chatting and laughing to and from school, you hardly saw any children in the streets at all."

Some children, already suffering shock and home-sickness, found it hard to settle down. Catherine Newberry was evacuated with her mother and four-year-old brother: "...to a little village in South Wales. When we were introduced to the woman of the house she looked at me and said: "I really wanted a girl of 14 to look after the children." We stayed there for a miserable and cold six weeks, then my Dad found us lodgings near his base."

But other children stayed in their new homes and even enjoyed the change of life-style. Some kept in touch for years with their temporary adoptive parents.

When the threatened air raids failed to happen in the autumn of 1939, many children were fetched home again so that by January 1940, about half the official evacuees were back with their families. Another wave of evacuation began when the Blitz started in September the same year.

Children left behind on the Island in war-time were in a changed world – the battles of "Boy's Own" suddenly became real. Bill O'Neill again:

"Came the 1939 crisis...we were kept busy filling sandbags for the Anderson air-raid shelters we were all putting in our small back gardens. All the factories were very busy, including the docks. It was a different Millwall now, especially with the black-out in operation.

All of the schools were taken over by the various civil defence forces, so our schooling was down to two or three mornings a week, in St.Mildred's House, so for the first time I was going to school with my "Proddie" (i.e. Protestant) mates. As boys, our new headquarters was the surface air raid shelter in St.Mildred's Square, and we defended it from gangs from over the bridge and the Hesperus Crescent gangs usually led by Dodger Porter. We used to have some right old stone-throwing battles until a window was broken, when within seconds there was not a soul to be seen.

The summer of 1940 brought Dunkirk. I remember going up to the Pier Head, that was over the bridge and turn left before the donkey field opposite the Seaman's Mission and the *Dock House* pub, to see the flotillas of small boats going down the Thames to Dunkirk. We really did not know what it was all about but understood a bit more when they were coming back, especially when some of the larger craft had wounded on board and soldiers lining their decks. We had one or two warships coming into the docks for repair."

After many false warnings, the raids came to East London on Saturday September 7th, 1940. In that first bombardment, thousands of homes were destroyed, 430 civilians were killed, and 1,600 seriously injured. After many rehearsals, the fire-fighters, rescue workers and first aiders were now called into action. But there had been no rehearsal for the frightening intensity of the bombing. Some people had already left. Now many more fled, by any means available, taking whatever belongings they could carry. Bill O'Neil's family left too:

"The raid (on September 7th) started about 4 o'clock and finished about five-thirty. Millwall was alight, there was no gas, water or electricity, but in true East End tradition a way was found to make a cup of tea. A stand pipe produced water and the local ladies queued for dad to boil their kettles using his welding torch. My mother queued for her turn and when her kettle boiled she took it into the living room and poured the boiling water around the cracks in the hearth because she heard a cricket down there and they were considered unlucky indoors. I can't

HMS Middleton, destroyer used on the arctic convoys - the Russian run. On board, leading gunner Frank Sale, of Stebondale Street.

remember if my dad swore or not!

The raiders returned about eight o'clock and left early next morning. I remember coming out of Le Bas gates and being amazed to see our houses still standing. I also vividly remember walking down to see the remains of St.Cuthbert's church, but I cannot remember what we had to eat those first three or four days of the blitz, we must have had something.

After two more nights of heavy bombing dad decided enough was enough so he somehow got hold of an open-back lorry and driver from Le Bas, loaded what family he could get on board with what we could carry and set off to our relations in Becontree...the journey from the Island took over five hours and when we arrived at Aunt Lizzie's there was a large saucepan of home-made vegetable soup on the go. I can still remember the taste and smell of that."

Harry Easter was just 15 when he and his family were forced to leave for good, as he recalled here:

"It was at the start of the Blitz. A fire bomb attack. There were three or four of us putting buckets of sand over some that had started in the street. I was 15. We had a shelter in the garden, but we thought we had better do something about the fires, we just came out on our own, there were buckets of sand all over the place, left on doorsteps, or earth – anything we could get hold of. At the back of 599 Manchester Road was the Dock Master's House, if I remember rightly their trees were afire, I was over there with another chap, we were chopping down these trees, and this fellow said, "Oh, look, there's the house on fire, I think it's Easter's", and I looked up, and it was! So I came round to the front of the house, and the top was then well ablaze, and I thought I'd try to see what I could rescue. There were areas (basement steps) and we used the back scullery because there was a brick boiler built in the corner and a bath there and we had a drawer with all the cutlery in it. I whipped up to one of the bedrooms, got a pillow case and put all the cutlery in it. I came out and turned round and realised my friend Stan Walker, he lived in a shop by *The Queen*, he was alongside me, helping

Members of the auxiliary services "making do" with temporary cooking arrangements when the gas and electricity had been cut off.

me. He was about my age, too. And then I saw my mother and two of my sisters standing outside the front of the house and I said, "Look, Mum, I've saved the silver.

She said, "Well, can you get us some warm coats?" because it was getting a bit chilly. So Stan and I rushed back into the house and up to the wardrobe and got their warm coats out. The firemen by that time had arrived with the Green Goddess (fire engine) and they were playing water on the house. The water was filtering down through the floors on to us, I remember how warm it felt because it had got heated by the fire, and I could hear the lumps of masonry falling onto the area steps and I can still hear those lumps falling down. By then we had got tin hats from somewhere. Then we realised the house was a write-off, it was so far ablaze, we just stood there for

a while in bewilderment that they dare to do that to us, then we turned away and made our way to my married stepsister living in Becontree. Now that was hairy too, because the buses were all up the creek, we went by a very circuitous route, and I still can't remember how we got there. In those days streets would be blocked off. It was a terrible feeling. I realised then – we'd seen pictures of refugees on the Continent with their bundles of clothing, and it suddenly struck home to me, we were like that, we had nothing except the clothes on our backs and a pillowcase full of cutlery.

We got to my stepsister's and she opened the door and looked at my mother and sisters and me and they all burst into tears and hung on each other's necks. Then we started a new life, got an empty house and started a new life."

In addition to the official evacuation, many families organised their own move to safer areas, returning whenever it seemed safe to do so. Mrs Bennett, of Cahir Street, was married with a little girl and her husband was in the Army:

"I evacuated to Somerset first and it stopped bombing and I said to him, I'll come home. Well, we came home and then it started again and he said, You'd better go back." She went to Oxfordshire and was close to her two sisters-in-law; they all found local cleaning jobs. But she didn't like the area: "It's out in the wilds, full up with water. I'm going home" and she came back. "The whole lot of us and we never went away no more".

Forced moves changed the direction of lives. Lilian Simmons spent her teenage years on the Island in the 1930s and she said: "I loved every minute of it. I worked in Godfrey Phillips tobacco factory in Commercial Street where I made many friends. When we had had a very bad night's bombing my dad came home for a short time and told us that we had to just leave and go to Oxford which is where my sisters had been evacuated to. My mum and I didn't want to leave our lovely house, as we had lived in cramped rooms for so long. As an eighteen-year-old I didn't want to go because I had a very nice boy friend. My Dad said, It will only be for a couple of weeks. I hated it at first, but I had to do as I was told." Lilian married an Oxfordshire man and settled there.

The war-time diary of young Arthur Mather gives a dramatic account of what the Blitz felt like at the time, and records the destruction of many Island landmarks. Here is an extract starting with the first day of bombing:

"It was a lovely afternoon and the sky was clear when the siren gave off the warning, which was followed soon after by the sound of aircraft. We stood outside the shelter and saw the big formation of planes coming towards us...puffs of bursting anti-aircraft shells were soon around them, by this time the planes were overhead and were turning a little to the left and then for the first time we heard the scream

of bombs falling...we laid on the floor of the shelter whilst every bomb that came near would send a splitting tearing wrench through the earth, which in its turn would shake the shelter. My first impulse was to run, but we stuck it, indeed, we could do nothing else, about two dozen bombs fell in about ten minutes, the worst ten minutes I have had or hope to have.

...we climbed out of the shelter. The sky looked as though it was on fire, the Surrey docks was ablaze from end to end, in fact the flames were about 400 yards high and the fire stretched nearly a mile along the river edge, blazing barges were floating with the tide, the wharves from which they were moored are now blazing ruins...

The Islanders public house was hit, Doctor Hackett's had a time bomb in it which went off and blew the whole block of houses to hell, Brown's butchers, sweet shop, Post Office and Dr Hackett's.

I went up to see my Gran she lives near Dr Hackett's, she was all right but I found the gas and electric was off and stopped all the work on the Island for a week, and the telephones are terrible...I walked back and along came a warden on a cycle, seeing my tin hat shouted "Give a warning, the raiders are over and there's no electricity to work the siren!" So I ran down the road, shouting, "Take Cover!"...the crackling of the fires on our side and the terrific fire that was raging in the Surrey Docks made you shout to make yourself heard...as I got to a firm nearly opposite where I live a watchman took me for a warden and shouted "The sparks from the other side of the river has set my wharf on fire".

My father and I, also a few neighbours, ran up to see if we could do anything to stop the fire and came up to the riverside. We could see the Surrey Docks fire, a gale blew the smoke down and nearly choked us. My father and I started to fight the fire, there were two motor fire pumps which we did not know how to work, anyway my father turned the handle and I pulled the plugs, suddenly the engine worked, we quickly fixed the hoses and put the jet on the fire, but we were drenched to the skin, the wind was blowing the spray back on us, by this time most of the buildings were afire on each side, Thames Oil Wharf, Lollar Wharf, were well ablaze and it looked as though our house in the main road might be in danger, you could hardly see or breathe when we got to our house, flaming sparks had set every garden afire, Goodrich's, French's, next door to us Hooper Cushen's, Still's the confectionery shop, were all alight, which my father and I put out, the time was now nine o'clock, and the bombs came screaming down, every time we would jump over the fences and

Elsie Wilde, of Millwall, joined the WAAF in the war and met Warrant Officer Robert Wright, who was in the RAF. In 1950 she went out to Singapore to marry him.

dive into the shelter... it was a night I think I will never forget....

(the raids continue) Saturday September 28th...the plane must have come out of the sun for the spotters never saw it, the place fairly rocked, we dashed to the shelters, it was a dreadful moment, three bombs fell in the river, one hit Kemball Bishops, one the *Dock House* pub, which with the coffee shop next door are in ruins....

March 19th 1941:..Millwall and Poplar had a few hundred high explosives and also incendiaries, Bullivant's shelter was hit and 70 out of 100 people were killed the rest were injured. St.Andrew's Wharf had a direct hit by high explosive bomb which went into an oil tank, which exploded and burning oil was blown hundreds of yards up into the sky....the wharves along West Ferry Road were alight, Morton's riverside wharf received a high explosive and a great

Visitors from the United States of America examining bomb damage in Garford Street.

amount of damage was done to that part of the factory that was not burnt out a few months ago. Glengall Grove received a great number of high explosives, one dropped outside the Isle of Dogs School, which blew all the cottages opposite and damaged them, the school burst into flame and was soon a blazing mass...A great many of the bombs fell in the docks and up in Poplar, the gas works were hit in Poplar, Chrisp Street had a quarter of the shops burnt out, Poplar passenger station was burnt out. The walls in Westferry Road were hit just before the second bridge and steel girders were flung across the road into the dock walls."

Dr.Blasker was also bombed out of his home in 1940. He moved to Manchester Grove, and stayed on the Island, caring for his patients and working in the air raid shelters night and day, throughout the war.

Taking shelter and keeping some kind of a home together, were priorities for every family still on the

Island. Corrugated iron "Anderson" shelters were distributed to households with space in their gardens. Public shelters were created in the basements of large buildings, or new ones were erected to serve groups of houses. People found their own safe places. On the Island, these were the railway arches in Millwall Park, and the crypt beneath Christ Church. Another favourite was Chislehurst caves, where Tilly Soper sheltered with her mother:

"Every night she used to say, "Are you coming, Till?" I would say, "Yes Mum." We would take the bed clothes. Away we would go through Greenwich

Public air-raid shelter at the Baths in Tiller Road

St.Cuthbert's Church, Westferry Road, after the first night of the Blitz in September 1940.

subway and then we would get the train at Greenwich station, then it would take us right to Chislehurst. We used to go about five, get there about half-past-six. Then we would be there all night and then Mum and I would leave about five o'clock in the morning."

The first wave of raids continued for 76 consecutive nights apart from a break on November 2nd when bad weather prevented flying. There were also daylight raids, and altogether this "Blitz" of raids continued for nine months, into the early summer of

1941. After that raids continued intermittently throughout the war and in 1945, in Cubitt Town, 75% of homes were found to be unfit for habitation. The population of the Island had shrunk from 21,000 to under 9,000. One third of all warehousing was destroyed, as were many public buildings, including community centres, pubs and churches.

"Early in the war St.Cuthbert's, Millwall, near St.Mildred's, was bombed and the congregation began to meet for services in St.Mildred's chapel. More than once bombs set alight the great timber stacks at the dock edge and the window sills of St.Mildred's became red hot from the fires. Once the street opposite became a hot stream of peanut butter when a bomb hit a neighbouring warehouse and for weeks, boots and carpets were saturated with the strong-smelling substance. Finally a flying bomb fell within the dock gates and St.Mildred's walls were split from top to bottom." (*Church Times, 1946*)

The Clergy House of St.John's Church in Manchester Road was destroyed in the night of March 19th to 20th, 1941. The official Report of the incident stated:

"The 250 kg bomb made a direct hit on the Clergy House in the Church Grounds. The Clergy House was completely demolished and considerable damage was done to other buildings nearby (which had previously suffered damage by bombing).

The School Building, owing to repeated incidents, now comes under Class B. The Main Building (St.John's Church) is structurally sound except the North Isle (sic) and Vestry, which will have to be rebuilt...5 People were sheltering and escaped injury (in a Steel Shelter 15 feet from the Clergy House).

All Houses in the immediate neighbourhood Cleveland Terrace, Roserton Street, East Ferry Road, Manchester Road, Chipka Street, have suffered severe damage in previous incidents which makes it impossible to state accurately to which date the Damage belongs. (All Residents evacuated prior to this incident.)"

The anti-aircraft guns which had been installed on the Mudchute were constantly in use, their noise rather comforting to hear, but they attracted the attention of the enemy planes, as a bomb report for the night of 27th to 28th December, 1940, shows:

"...at 10 minutes past 10, a 50 kg bomb fell on the anti-aircraft battery at the back of Stebondale Street... bomb fell outside the 30-foot diameter reinforced concrete gun emplacement, penetrated underneath same, completely wrecking foundations and demolishing

Top picture opposite: Colin and Ken Hunter, 1947, in the garden of 27 Malabar Street, with the air-raid shelter still in place.

Lower picture opposite: Soldiers of the 154th battery 52nd HAA, at the Mudchute gun-site, which has been damaged by a bomb.

surrounding 12-inch thick 5 feet 6 inches high wall. Gun damaged. Note: the gun was undergoing repairs at time of incident and was not in use."

Page after page of bomb reports illustrate the relentless bombardment of the Island. The night of the 19th to 20th February 1941 is just one example, when, between 10 minutes to 10 and half-past 10, bombs fell outside 38-40 Chapel House Street, damaging a gas main; on 431-433 Westferry Road, causing serious damage, on numbers 7, 9, 11 and 13 Hesperus Crescent, seriously damaging all four of these "council cottages" and the road outside; on the Isle of Dogs Treatment Centre in Harbinger Road "already damaged in previous raid"; and on the junction of Glengall Grove and Alpha Grove, causing damage to council houses, the school and Island Baths."

Meanwhile the Island's factories were being battered. One night, three 50kg bombs fell on Sternol Ltd., at Grosvenor Wharf. "Bombs fell on three-storey, steel framed brick building with reinforced concrete floors. This was demolished and set on fire by explosions but was quickly got under control. Adjoining building under repairs from previous bombing also badly damaged.

…and at the same time, five incendiary bombs fell on Maconochie Brothers in Westferry Road: Incendiary bombs fell on Can Stores. One failed to ignite. three Bays of 1st storey building 85 feet long and 25 feet wide were destroyed by fire. Steel framed roofs with wood purlins, partially glazed and slated were completely wrecked. Outside walls remained intact." (Bomb Reports)

The East Ferry Crane and Engineering Works had supplied hydraulic cranes to the Port of London Authority in the late 1920s and early 1930s. It also made pneumatic grain elevators which were marketed throughout the world. The works were bombed in the war and the firm moved to Rainham, where it stayed until closure in 1974.

Production continued wherever possible. Lucy Reading, who worked at C. & E.Morton's throughout the Blitz, recalled how everyone would take shelter, and have a sing-song: "One half was singing *Pack Up Your Troubles in Your Old Kit-Bag*, and the other half was singing *It's a Long Way to Tipperary*…you would try and drown the noise out. Then the "All Clear" would go and we would go back to work."

Describing one incident, she said: "We went to work one day and Morton's had been alight, and oh, they were black, the firemen, eyes down to their cheekbones, absolutely shattered. One of them had a nasty cut on his hand, it was black and it was just bleeding, but they were taking no notice of that… And then we were allowed to go in and have a look at the damage to our own department… where they had used the hoses on the fire, everything was wet. There was this tall stack of trays of chocolates, and a great big lump of shrapnel had gone right the way through, through the whole lot. So it all had to be taken away

and disposed of. And the ground was sticky and wet because of the sugar…Work carried on the next day, you didn't get any time off. They found something for you to do."

Samuel Cutler's, with other similar firms, did a great deal of Government work. Besides repairs to bombed gas holders, they worked on landing craft, gun turrets, contracts for the RAF and other projects. Their premises suffered two High Explosive bombs and their Home Guard post was destroyed, but they stayed open.

Some factories were completely destroyed, like the Star Pram and Mangle Factory. Some, like Manganese Bronze, makers of ships' propellers, moved away (in their case to Birkenhead); others patched up the damage and carried on. Hawkins and Tipson's rope works were hit:

"In 1940 our Blackwall mill, wharf and warehouses were destroyed by enemy bombers in September. "A" Mill and the main hemp warehouse were also burnt down. Thousands of bales of fibre were destroyed, we were down to only 25% output for a time and our claims for fibre alone amounted to £73,000. Fortunately we obtained a site at Edmonton large enough to replace the Blackwall factory, but these premises were not at the water side so we were no longer able to land our raw materials. The binder twine machines from Blackwall, which were not badly damaged, were accommodated by Green Brothers of Hailsham, where they were running by the end of February 1941. Later we had many bombs on various parts of the Millwall factory and temporary repairs had to be carried out."(*Company history*)

Snowdon Sons & company, the oil blenders, moved their offices to Crawley for the duration of the war, and when it was over took new offices in Buckingham Palace Road – though their Island works continued to operate.

The Port made its own contribution to the war effort. In the early months trade fell noticeably. The river was mined by the Germans and could not be used for shipping until the navy developed the minesweeper. Then, with German troops in France, shipping was diverted away from London to safer ports. However, the docks and ship-repair yards remained open and active throughout the war. Dockers were mobilised for war work and sent where they were needed. An entire contingent of London dockers spent the war in Scotland. Harry Anderson went to Cardiff:

"We got sent down to Cardiff. You see, the reason why there was so many London members sent to the west coast, there was so many ships getting torpedoed in the Channel and the approaches to the Channel, the English Channel, they diverted the ships round to the west coast. Well they never did have a vast army of men down there working in the docks, so there was all this extra work, they wanted more men. You had lease and lend cargo (sic), and shiploads of meat from

War-time wedding at Christ Church for Maureen Marson and Frank Pritchard. Also in the picture, Frank's parents, David Marson, Lily Wilson, George Wilson, Eileen Brooker, Doreen Welsh, Beatrice Ross, Eileen Ross, David and Valerie Ross and Valerie Wilson.

New Zealand, to be put into cold storage. They sent four hundred and fifty men up there, some went to Cardiff, some to Barry, some to Newport, some to Penarth, some to Swansea, and I was sent to Cardiff, I was up there for fourteen weeks."

The ship-repair yards mended naval and mercantile vessels of all kinds, and the "Mulberry" harbours were fabricated in the East India and Surrey Docks. On 6th June 1944 a great flotilla of 209 ships, 194 of them loaded in the docks, together with 1,000 barges, sailed down the Thames to "take part in the greatest amphibious assault in history". (Pudney).

The docks were a prime target and a summary of just one page of many bomb reports gives an inkling of what a night's work was like for the fire-fighters and bomb disposal units. On the night of 19th to 20th April 1941, between midnight and four o'clock, 58 bombs, mainly 50 kg, fell on the East and West India and Millwall Docks, damaging or destroying timber, sheds, railway tracks, hydraulic mains, a tackleman's store, offices, silos, bridges, roadways, footpaths, quaysides and warehousing, some of which had already been damaged in previous raids.

Under wartime conditions, some sort of life had to go on, with more hardship than previously, but also with a greater determination and a greater need to achieve some kind of normality, maintain customs and basic comforts.

Although some schools were too badly damaged to function, and others were taken over by the auxiliary services, some, St.Luke's being one, remained open. The log book for the period reveals a tale of constant interruptions for air raids, testing of gas masks, shelter exercises and teacher shortages, whilst the school roll rose and fell according to the intensity of the raids. Terse entries suggest teachers carrying on in spite of difficulties: "16.6.44. Air raid alert still on at 9.30 a.m. attendance 12 children. alert at 1p.m. all clear 1.30 approx. alert 1.55 all clear 2.50 attendance 17 children and full staff."

Weddings were more popular than ever in wartime, in spite of the prospect of long separations, rationing and uncertainty about finding a home. George Thurgar recalled: "We were married in Christ Church. It was the height of the flying bombs, 1944. The vicar said, I will give you a very curtailed service and if the warning goes while you are being married, get back under the pews. We were lucky. We walked back to Thermopylae Gate and we got opposite Maconochies before the warning went."

Rationing was a fact of life – cardboard wedding cakes became fashionable – and since most Islanders had been more or less "rationed" in the amount of food they could eat, beer they could drink, clothes they could buy, for most of their lives, war-time restrictions were no surprise, though scarcity and queuing were new.

Mrs Stevens recalled that: "People would knock on the door and say, "They've got liver this morning, don't forget to be there. And oranges were unheard of, you know. But if you got liver you was very, very lucky."

Getting supplies to the Island was a problem because transport was badly disrupted. The pre-war local traditions whereby you could "get almost anything in the pub", the custom of buying and selling on a no-questions-asked basis, provided the foundations on which the war-time black market could flourish for those who wanted it. "Talking about black market: they had it off to a fine art, didn't they? Petrol coupons that people couldn't get. I know someone that's got two or three hundred they wanted to sell, got to pay about three times over the odds for it, coupons, people can't get sugar, I know

Joyce and Lucy Humphries, of Galbraith Street, in 1939. When their home was destroyed, they moved to Downham with their parents and sister Rose. The house there received a direct hit, killing Joyce and Lucy, their mother and father, and the aunt and cousin they were staying with. Rose returned from work to find all her family dead.

someone who's got some sugar, you could hear it all over the place… "

Those shops that managed to stay open during the Blitz had a struggle to survive rationing, as goods were scarce and as their customers were getting fewer. Mr Huish, owner of the haulage firm, considered that: "Many shopkeepers who had been a lifetime in business in this area were forced by circumstances to close down as the war progressed"

Meat for human consumption was rationed and "the cat's meat man" who had been a feature of pre-war street life, disappeared altogether. Pets were abandoned or put down. Mrs Stevens remembered that: "All the cats and dogs had to go. People came round – going on evacuation and that, they all had their animals put down. Had a gorgeous Alsatian next door but one, that had to go, my Mum's two cats went, you went to the lady and they came and took them."

Human casualties were high, every individual story a personal tragedy. Mrs Anderson's husband worked in the docks, he was a stevedore. No longer young, he and his wife had evacuated to Leighton Buzzard. but he: "… got fed up with this and said he could do more up in London than he could here, he was up here a fortnight and that was it, he got killed. He was only home a fortnight. Just before eight one morning, he said, I'll see you just before 12, I said, Right-oh, he gets halfway down the dock, three lorries of Canadian soldiers behind him…down came the bomb and killed the lot. We didn't know until seven o'clock at night."

Rescue workers had to deal with death and injury on a large scale, often being in the front line themselves. Connie Cox recorded: "Bill Cox, my husband, was in Cubitt Town School when it had a direct hit with a land mine. He was the most seriously injured of the five they got out alive. We never knew how many were killed, the young telephonist was never found. This was in September 1940, it was a First Aid Post and AFS Station."

Dennis Dawson's father, a lighterman, had joined the Civil Defence: "The reason he took this job was that no ships were coming into our docks, they were going to Hull and Liverpool and so there was no money coming in to the home. He was in the section called CWD (Civilian War Dead). They had to collect the bodies of people killed in the air raids and take them to the mortuaries. This must have been a truly horrific job…but he never grumbled or spoke about what he was doing. I recall when I was in the army I was home on leave and I went to visit him where he was working and saw him hosing out the back of the vehicle they had used after a raid. It was obvious from the colour of the water why it was being washed out."

The exact loss of human life in the Island community may never be known. In addition to the recorded civilian dead and the fatalities amongst the Home Guard and other auxiliary services, many

End of Second World War: Peace Party in Malabar Street, Millwall.

members of the armed forces from the Island died in battle.

Jim Edmonds was one of eight, five sisters and three brothers. One of his brothers: "...lived on the Island and he got married younger than me, and he got killed in the navy in March 1945, at Dieppe. He was in the engine room when they got blasted and he got out but he died on the way to hospital. He is buried in Dieppe...he was the youngest one of all, he was 22 when he got killed. And his wife...went to live with my mother in Manchester Road and then she suddenly developed TB and she died of a broken heart."

Alf French felt his mother had died of exhaustion and shock: "When she died she was quite worn out, she was worn out, she was an old lady in her fifties. I was away, during the war of course I was away, in the Eighth Army, but she died during the war largely as a result of the shock of a bomb, a bomb on the house, she was in the shelter but the house was ruined, this shocked her but another shock which came only a week or so after that was that my brother was killed in the war, and the shock of these two things, she just died."

Jessie Diss married Fred Gofton in 1940 and they lived in Macquarie Way. Fred's brother Harry was killed at El Alamein in 1943. Fred was killed in 1944 whilst working on a Lancaster bomber and Jessie's sister was killed by a V2 rocket in the same year.

George Thurgar was in the Navy. Looking back he considered himself lucky:

"I dodged practically everything. I was in the last convoy to get out of Narvick. The Germans were using Narvick when we were going there. The last time I was there, just after we sailed from Narvick, the Germans went on shore. I had been to Norway three times and never set foot on Norwegian soil... I got out

of Narvick all right, then I came ashore and had a hernia operation, and just as soon as I left the ship, she struck a mine. Two people got killed. Then the next ship I was on for a couple of trips, I saw on the Memorial in Tower Hill, the name of the ship and she must have got sunk with nearly all hands. There were about 47 names on there. Then there was another ship I was on called the *Dorset*, and she was in the very famous Malta Convoy, where four ships got through out of fourteen, and she was one of the ten that didn't get through. She was the last one to get sunk before she got to Malta. No one got killed, but she sank. I was on that one about eight months before, so all in all I was lucky. I went to Malta the following convoy after that and we were only attacked by one plane. I consider myself very lucky, compared to what some of them went through....".

And when George and people like him came back, it wasn't the Island, and it wasn't the life, they had left behind. They had been in other places, seen other things and they were no longer the boys who had gone away. Bernie Bannister reflected on this:

"Things were very slow, getting back from the war. People were picking themselves up, you know. They were going from one life to another, as I did. If I went out I wouldn't go across a field, I would stick to the paths...because I was mine conscious, because it had happened to me, not once but three or four times. I lost blokes who were killed by mines. This is the sort of thing you've got, you know. And you are out of the army one minute and then you are back in the docks. A lot of blokes were the same, so life was very very slow picking up...picking up that job afterwards I found it so different. A different world...but I suppose you eventually get settled down."

7. The Island environment

Catherine Taylor described the post-war years as: "...a period of great change, a sad time, nearly every family had lost someone – a husband, father, son or uncle – and everyone was striving to make a home. There was, however, a great feeling of neighbourliness and friendship. On summer evenings the Mums would sit and chat on the window sills and the children played happily in the streets – skipping, hopscotch, or with whip and top."

Islanders recovered some of the rythmns of their pre-war life, but the war had permanently altered the old streets. The Victorian terraces had disappeared or remained as shells of brickwork, with here and there an inhabited house. Housing built between the wars had also suffered bomb damage. Shops had been blasted away or were shuttered and closed, the surviving pubs stood out like ancient monuments, others had vanished leaving only a pile of rubble. Churches were destroyed or cracked and broken, schools were damaged or gone altogether. Some of the bombed wharves and factories had been repaired or rebuilt, but other companies had closed down or moved to safer areas. Acres of prefabricated houses were a new feature and everywhere there were heaps of debris and the activities of patching, mending and repainting."

Student artist Kathleen Hyndman wandered round the Island during the winter of 1948-49, writing notes and making sketches for her undergraduate thesis. In Manchester Road she saw: "...terraced houses – bombed...the bombed houses had sightless eyes of windows...here and there a house in use, so repainted and lonely among the empty shells on either side. In front of the houses were dark grey plane trees with nearly dead leaves, under one were four children rolling in the dust...It all seemed more strange and unreal as the dusk approached. I explored the turnings to my left; in one stood the *Newcastle Arms*, at the top of a short grey uphill road, smoke-begrimed houses, many uninhabited... The pub itself was newly painted, bright and isolated, its vividness made more startling by the completely grim surroundings... I passed Cubitt Town, an extensive area of flat cream prefabs, squarely laid out midst grey unpainted Belisha beacons. Opposite was the Sterling Mangle Works. There are no shops in this part of the Island – little life. further on were a group of children, men knocking off work... More terrace houses, each with a dustbin by the front door..."

Kathleen described the local children as

Jacobs sheep and the old gun-site on the Mudchute with Christ Church in the background, 1970s.

specialising in: "...that blackness of visage that comes through damp faces and grubby hands, they are all lovable bright and eager and like all children, have that unimpeachable sense of justice." Her impression of the Island was of grime, dullness, damage and windiness, offset by the sun sparkling on the river, flaming red evening skies, the friendliness of the inhabitants and the splashes of colour from new paintwork.

In 1959 when she was a student midwife, Diana Waters spent six months on the Island and later recalled: "...the first thing that struck me was the atmosphere of the place. The water and the boats predominated. The docks were still operating; barges

St. John's Church, destroyed in the Blitz. Photograph from National Monuments Record.

and ships moved through the vast open expanse of water; the bridges were frequently raised; the Island was still in a state of devastation. Recalling an early morning birth, she wrote: "We left the house at 4.30a.m. It was getting light, the sky was beautiful as the sun rose – orange, with a pink tinge. You could smell the water and the boats, hear the sounds of tugs, sirens and chains; otherwise, it was quiet."

There were still free goodies for children; one Islander remembered: "the barges, roped in line from the shore out in the river, at Newcastle Drawdock...

the peanut barge was always furthest out." And another memory was of the "sugar lorries" and the trick of slitting the bags when the lorry stopped and gathering up the spilt sugar.

Tony Hale remembered the smell: "that over-sickly sweet peanutty aroma that drifted out of the British Oil and Cake Mills wharves, workshops and packing areas. It was cattle cake that they processed and packed...but to a teenager it was just another mystery of the river; the barges sailing up and down, the little police launches scurrying back and forth, and the never-ending line of blackened hulls of the tramps that creaked their way up the river towards the Pool."

The "debris" – the rubble of homes and schools and shops – dominated the landscape... Margaret Turpin said: "If you went anywhere, you'd say, I'm going across the debris because it literally was, going across the debris. The children went across the debris, or you would find the children playing on the debris, because there was nothing there." And she also remembered: "...nothing to see except flames where they had set fire to a house, or they were pulling it down," as the clearance got under way.

The shells of a ruined building in Glengall Grove (now Tiller Road) was a camp for young George Pye and his friends: "...climbing up the outside of the building, to go in our camp. That was the elite – no-one went up there – only the idiots. It was an outside drain pipe and you had to climb up there to be initiated, I suppose. And the camp was right up in the rafters. They laid boards and bits and pieces and it was a camp. Had a fire down below in a bungalow-type building which was probably an air raid shelter...they used to cook and things like that in there. Looking at it now, it was very, very dangerous I suppose – but the only person we were putting in danger was ourselves."

And if the debris and the bomb sites, the tumbling houses and cracked and broken warehouses, the rationing and the strangeness of it all, were not enough, there was the Cold War to contend with. Poplar Borough Council *Tenants' Handbook* for the 1950s reminded readers that: "...we have to face the constant threat that this world and this country in particular will be suddenly plunged into nuclear warfare with all its attendant horrors and destruc-tion." The closest the Island came to this was on the 9th December, 1953, when an exercise by the Civil Defence Experimental Mobile Column tested the conveyance of their personnel by water on a mission to rescue and evacuate casualties of an atomic attack. Twenty casualties with fake injuries took part and were taken on board a boat at Newcastle Drawdock on the Isle of Dogs. Reporters and photographers

Top picture opposite: The lead works, Westferry Road, with River Thames and Greenwich.

Lower picture opposite: West Ferry Road and Christ Church in 1954.

were in attendance as were a few curious Islanders.

There was still plenty of work locally in the 1950s and 1960s, still the long walk of "the walls" and "the bridgers" to negotiate in order to go shopping or "up West". Kathy Weir (nee Bates), who lived in the Fire Station cottages, wrote: "Often my father and I would walk all the way to Deptford Market on a Saturday..." and Ursula Marchant remembered: "dreadful smogs when we had to walk all the way to Mile End Station because the buses had stopped running." When it was fine, children enjoyed the walk to Greenwich Park: "running through the subway and up the other side". Peter Wright recalled that there were just four cars in the whole of Tooke Street in the 1950s, including his dad's Austin 30. People still walked or cycled to work – but wages and living standards were rising and as local public transport remained unreliable, by the 1960s 40% of Island families owned a car, compared with 27% for East London as a whole.

Millwall Park and George Green's playing field, in the background, McDougall's Mill and silos, cranes and shipping in the Millwall Docks; the Mudchute banks are visible above the roof of the rope walk.

The authorities, who were faced with an enormous task of post-war reconstruction, were slow to deal with the Island and it was neglected. "The forgotten Island" Councillor John Vicat called it in the 1950s. The baths had not been rebuilt, the Glengall Road bridge over the Millwall Dock had not been repaired. In spite of the building of low-rise flats and maisonettes in the St.John's and Alpha Grove areas in the late 1940s and early 1950s, there was still overcrowding, poor housing, bomb sites and prefabs in many places. All these problems were discussed on the streets and in the pubs and factories, and were the stimulus for the formation of groups such as Alpha Old Age Pension Association, founded in 1948 by John McDonald, who was also a member of Poplar Borough Council.

School provision was outdated and run-down. St.Edmund's school was: "A Victorian building, it had outside toilets and a large bell high up in the roof...In the ground floor hall there was a huge open fireplace where, in the winter, if you wanted your bottle of milk warmed, it was placed in front of a blazing fire", wrote Kathy Weir, who started school in 1954.

Shopping facilities on the Island were "among the poorest in East London" – many shops had been destroyed and remaining shopkeepers found it a struggle to pay the high rates demanded for new shops. Later came the threat of competition from new chains and supermarkets. Maggie Gleeson kept on the family shop (see Chapter 2) after her father died in the war. During the 1950s she learned to do invisible mending and she also made aprons and overalls. Trade picked up again and takings averaged about £25 a week. The shop provided the family with enough to live on – anything over was put back into the business. In 1960 Maggie was given notice to quit,

Harry Wright, Peter Wright and John Nichols outside No.4, Tooke Street, a prefab, in 1956. Peter Wright recalled the road surface made of concrete sections "many a time I tripped on the joins in my skates, and now realise it was used to fill in the bomb craters." There were only four cars in the street at this time.

and moved into what had been an oil shop in Manchester Road, next to the Police Station. There was living accommodation above, and an outside toilet in the back yard. They cleaned the place up and stayed there 10 years, until a compulsory purchase order forced them out. Maggie moved to a newly-built shop opposite Christ Church until she retired to a flat close by.

Absence of motor traffic meant that children could still play in the streets, go out on errands and enjoy the secure and quiet environment in other ways, much as in pre-war days:

"I can remember...us both being sent to Harry Saunders, the butcher, every Saturday morning. His shop was where the George Green outside play areas are now. This errand was a treat, as Harry would give us each a slice of spam to chew. Afterwards we used to go to Saturday morning pictures over at Greenwich, sixpence each to get in and threepence to spend. I also remember shows for us kids in Island Gardens during the summer holidays and spending ages playing in the paddling pool in Millwall Park." (Kathy Weir, talking about the early 1960s)

Sheila Batten recalled: "...we still had George, the Express Dairy milkman delivering by horse and cart, also Price's bread man with either a hand barrow or his horse-drawn cart. I can remember the first bread-man to deliver by motorised vehicle – it was the Co-op with a small red van.

We all played in the street, traffic was non-existent, maybe the ice-cream man with his pedal-trike twice a day in the summer and the man with a roundabout on the back of his horse and cart, who gave us a ride for either an old ha'penny or a one-pound jam jar. On Sundays there was Ike Emms with his hand cart, selling winkles and shrimps for our Sunday tea."

By the 1960s the streets were busier, but not so busy that the film *Sparrows Can't Sing* could not be made in and around Millwall. According to local memory, the film crew was "always surrounded by children" and they used some of them as extras.

One Island tradition which continued after the war was keeping pigeons. On light evenings and at weekends, flocks of pigeons could be seen circling overhead, and during the race season, children were enlisted as runners. Marion Hesselden (nee Burton) remembered how, on Fridays, she helped her father Alf (Nobby) to take his birds to the club, which was in the *North Pole* then: "When the birds were ringed, registered and put into baskets, they were put into lorries to be taken to the place of liberation. All the pigeon clocks were set and sealed, the owners would have a pint or two and us kids would have a glass of lemonade and a penny arrowroot biscuit. On Saturday morning it was my job to go to a house on the corner of Mellish Street, where they had a telephone and could take all the details of the liberation time, wind direction, etcetera. and these were chalked up on a board outside. I used to run all the way home repeating this information to myself, and Dad gave me sixpence for this. The garden was out of bounds until all the birds came home and were clocked in. The clocks were then taken to the club and opened, the results eagerly awaited, for quite a lot of prize money was at stake."

Very slowly, over the three decades following the end of the Second World War, a new Island landscape

Les Crane's newsagents and tobacconists shop in Westferry Road in the 1950s.

emerged from the damage. The high dock walls were still there and some of the bridges – though the bridge at the entrance to Millwall Dock had gone. Factories and wharves still lined the river's edge, though there were gaping holes. New streets of houses and blocks of flats and maisonettes appeared, rows of new small shops on the Barkantine, in Castalia Square and opposite Christ Church; the *Tooke Arms* was rebuilt and there was a new school, Seven Mills School, for Millwall. The ruined Island

David Bowen buying fruit in the street near his home in Hesperus Crescent in 1951. The fruit-seller came round every week, selling apples and oranges.

Baths were also rebuilt. The right-of-way over Millwall Dock was retained, after a local campaign, in the form of the "Glass Bridge" a high-level enclosed walkway, the mid-section of which could be raised to allow ships to pass. By 1977, following another vigorous local campaign, the Island had its own comprehensive school, the George Green Centre.

Danny, an Islander recalling his childhood in the 1970s, remembered traditional pastimes – playing in the street with a wooden go-kart, football round the garages: "we played for eight hours a day"; diving off the Glass Bridge and: "..we used to climb over the

walls, go along to different firms, have a look round...behind *The Vulcan* was a firm where you could go down the ladder to the river, and walk round to Poplar and back on the mud...had to rush back to avoid the tide". There was table tennis, snooker and judo at the Dockland Settlement, and street parties for the Silver Jubilee in 1977.

There were several new community centres, and John McDougall park had been opened to provide green space on the Barkantine Estate. New trees had been planted in the streets to replace the original London planes.

1977 was also the year the Mudchute began its new life as a community park and farm, combined with a flourishing Allotments Society. This was yet another success for community action which came about when, Islanders, including both old and new residents, retired dock workers and professionals, rallied to save the open space from a GLC housing development. After a well-organised campaign, the housing plans were dropped. Money was raised, the land was leased from the PLA, workers and volunteers were recruited and the Island acquired an important new resource, managed by local people.

The Island had become almost a green and pleasant place and it was becoming a quieter place. Grass was growing around old gateways and corrugated iron fences were appearing round deserted wharves and factories. The sounds of factory hooters and the rumble of machinery were diminishing. As the creeping economic decline spread to the West India and Millwall Docks, the cranes fell still and silent, the shipping disappeared, and the river was empty of traffic.

Evening Standard columnist Simon Jenkins described the Island in 1972 as "...an incredible place", with its "...wild open spaces and splendid views...the interior interlaced with the open water of the doomed docks.." and argued that Tower Hamlets Council should encourage private investment. Many minds were focussing on the question of how to revive the economy of the Island and the whole of the vast area of docks and run-down industry east of the Tower of London alongside the Thames. Players in the game included five London Boroughs, the Greater London Council and the Port of London Authority, the trade unions and numerous local organisations. There were plenty of carefully considered plans, but conflicting interests made progress difficult, and the decline continued.

When he arrived on the Island in 1976, Laurie Laken, sports instructor and writer of verse, found: "derelict docks, where cranes stand guard like sentries in an empty yard, deep murky water, floating planks, where rats and debris line its banks..."

By then, visions of what the future environment might be like were beginning to emerge within the community. Early in the 1970s, a writer in the church magazine, *Island Contact*, remarked prophetically:

"The trend is for firms to move off and the long term trend is to open up the river to the residents. That is something we welcome. What a dream it would be, imagine the whole water front, all round the island, fringed by a park and riverside walks, with trees and flowers. Maybe it will happen one day. It will be of benefit to London as well as to the Island, if it does."

Harry Anderson, who lived and worked on Island all his life, was interviewed in 1980 before redevelopment began. He said: "I've seen a lot of changes on this Island, I've seen so many firms closing down, the rates are exorbitant, on this Island, terrific...the rates have gone sky high, these firms can't stand it, so they just moved out...You walk round this Island you see hundreds of firms that have closed, the gates are still there, the factories are still there. I venture to say, in a few years' time, this Island will be solely residential."

Bill Price, of Kingfield Street, with his first car, in 1956. Also in the picture: Mike Shaw, Michael "Benny" Glander, Bert Franklin, Will Price, Janet Price and Pauline Price.

8. The Island at Work

In 1945, some Island firms had already relocated to other parts of the country and others had closed down altogether. Many which had survived found themselves locked into nineteenth-century premises, with cobbled access roads and narrow gateways, unsuited to modern machinery and transport. Building new industrial premises in East London was hindered by planning rules which favoured the separation of housing and manufacturing, and by rising rates. The docks and wharves had been badly damaged and were in urgent need of investment and modernisation,

In the 1950s and early 1960s, an underlying trend towards the decline of trade and industry on the Island was masked by brisk business during the post-war economic recovery. But gradually the effects of competition from abroad, from more efficient producers at home with access to faster transport, and from new docks with up-to-date cargo-handling methods, began to take their toll. The problems were felt most keenly in the Port. This was not a business which could simply move away to a new greenfield site outside the the capital, nor could the nineteenth century structure of the docks, with their traditional customs, easily be altered. The eventual closure of the up-river docks and wharves affected the manufacturing and service industries which were dependent on the Port of London Authority as customers for their goods and services, and for the transport and storage of their raw materials and finished products.

So the post-war picture of the Island's economy is again a mixed one, of failures, amalgamations, relocations, and the survival of the few. By the end of the 1970s, only a handful of the Island's old industrial giants remained, isolated amidst empty sites and the silent waters of the docks. Statistics collected by Cole (1981) illustrate the scale of change. Employment in London's docks fell from 31,000 in the mid-1950s to 9,800 in the mid-1970s; and in ship-building and ship-repair from 6,000 to less than 1,000 in the same period; barge traffic on the river declined from 13 million tons in 1963 to 3 million tons in 1978. On the Island, unemployment remained relatively low until the early 1970s, partly because of the general prosperity of the country and of the capital, and partly because of a falling population.

Some unemployment was always to be found in what was still a relatively poor area, but the figures rocketed in the 1970s. The number of jobs in Island firms declined by almost one-third, from 9,200 in 1969 to 6,200 in 1977; 60 per cent of job losses were in manufacturing, and most of the rest were in river and port transport work. At the same time the population was rising as big new estates, such as Barkantine and Samuda, were built and in 1977 unemployment was 16%, twice as high as for the country as a whole.

Not only the Island, but all the riverside communities east of the Tower were blighted by industrial decline and the general economic recession. According to Palmer (2000): "By the beginning of the 1970s, 10,000 workers were on the dole in Dockland north and south of the river... at the start of the following decade the jobless total for the same area had increased eight times over." And by then, the Government had intervened.

The events of the 1970s came as all the more of a blow to Islanders because they followed the prosperity of the 1950s and 1960s, when virtually full employment was supplemented by health and welfare systems which were a great improvement on anything which had existed pre-war.

Business in the port had soon picked up after the war. By 1949 British exports were 55 per cent up on the 1938 figure, a rapid recovery unmatched anywhere else in Europe. In what Palmer (2000) describes as: "a notable achievement by management and workers, the Thames recovered trade lost before and during the war, to Mersey and the Clyde. Only the East India Export Dock, damaged during the construction of the Mulberry Harbours, was abandoned and sold. The Brunswick Power Station, built on the site, revived a name familiar in eighteenth century Blackwall... The PLA could still claim to be the greatest port in the world. Tilbury was busy, but as late as 1958, so were the quays and wharves from Tower Bridge eastwards to the three Royals, handling the greatest volume of trade over any twelve months in their history."

W. Miller and C. Lambert outside the PLA workshop at the dock entrance near what is now Mudchute Station in East Ferry Road, 1950s.

Bernie Bannister remembered: "...and from about 1953 or 1955 the warehouses were being built, they put up these prefabricated tin sheds, things like that and we had a brand new office sent over from Sweden... they had sent special plans over, everything was in Swedish we couldn't read a word. Showers, they started coming in. Things we had never had before the war – canteen, the old PLA mobile canteen come round, it started getting better."

Talking about the busy years of the 1950s, barge-builder John Penn recalled that: "...the ships used to lay two abreast, side by side, waiting to be repaired or discharged, and the whole of the quay, say in the Albert Dock, very large dock, you could look all the way down the quay and you'd see a ship from one end of the dock to the other, a ship on either side of the dock all the way down, and some of them were laying two abreast. And some were even building new sheds. The United States Lines were building a new shed because of the amount of work they had."

Some of the younger dockers began to earn relatively good wages at this time, by comparison with the past: "In the 1950s... you would see all the young men with their cars and the lovely suits they used to

have. 'Course, the money was coming into the docks then", recalled Mrs Skinner.

With business booming there was new investment and new cargo-handling methods. Pudney relates how when work started at the Royal Docks after the war, it proved easier to use tractors and trailers on the rubble-strewn quays than to manipulate hand-barrows. Another legacy of the war was a few fork-lifts trucks, left by American forces. They were soon widely adopted and allowed goods to be moved more easily and quickly and with the use of pallets, warehouses could be stacked higher, and all with less manpower than previously. War-time shipments of tank-landing craft inspired the "roll-on, roll-off" system, where lorry-loads of goods went straight into the ship and out onto the road again at the port of destination. By the late 1960s there were more than 50 of these "RO-RO" services between Britain and the Continent and short sea traffic upstream from Tilbury had virtually stopped. Passenger liners, having lost custom to the airlines, became cruise ships and the Royal Docks ceased to be a major passenger terminal, although small cruise ships continued to use Millwall Dock.

Other changes were occurring. Road was taking over from rail in the transport of goods and so ports with good road connections had the advantage. Ships were getting larger and longer and operating costs were rising. Pressure was on to make the turn around faster so that less time was spent in port. Navigating the Thames upstream became increasingly tricky and costly. The East Coast ports, like Felixstowe, Harwich and Ipswich, with their easier access and lower costs, began to take cargo traffic away from London. Finally, containers appeared, with all their advantages. Containers cut out the need for handling individual units of cargo, and for secure warehousing.

Bernard Bannister remembered the shift towards Tilbury: "...they went to Tilbury, the Swedish boats went to Tilbury and the 26 berth there, which was better for them, really, because they could discharge and load on the 26 berth, round, out of the dock into Tilbury, pick up the passengers and away, save all that travelling up and down stream...and all these container works were coming in, it was all coming in fast and furious you see. But back up here (on the Island) we hadn't reached containerisation by then, ours was then pallets. Cargo ...was palletised to make a bulk fixed storage to whatever port you want it to."

The progress of change was uneven. In London and other major UK ports, the docks, warehousing and equipment were out-dated. The size of the workforce, and the cargo-handling system, all reflected traditional and time-consuming practices. George Pye started work in the Millwall Dock in

1954: Goods for export arriving by road at West India Dock, viewed from Nos. 10 and 11 ware-houses, looking westwards.

Quay Gang Foreman, 1953.

1960: "...Where Olsen's is today (1980) there was "P" and "J" sheds and they was the little nineteenth century sheds with little canopies outside, little landing stages, very low ceilings and then pulleys and the things in there! I mean, it was like a museum...the conditions you were in and the tools you were given to work with, was unbelievable. I couldn't believe what I was seeing...particularly as I was watching television indoors and things like that."

To bring the docks up-to-date, with a reduced labour force and streamlined cargo-handling facilities, required massive investment in new technology and redundancy payments for large sections of the workforce. This modernisation programme was an expense which threatened to cripple the London docks financially at a time when competition with European and other UK ports was becoming fiercer. Whilst improvements were slowly planned and implemented, other docks, with more space, with modern equipment and with good access to the motorways, were already taking the business away. A new grain terminal at Tilbury put an end to the useful life of the grain-handling facilities at Millwall and eventually to McDougalls flour mill in the Millwall Docks (Palmer).

Palletisation and containerisation meant that job losses were inevitable. George Pye recalled that between 1966 and 1970: "...we left the conventional cargo to palletise cargo, then we left that and come

home to container work...and the shipping-off gangs, there was eight men, the shipping-off gang, and thirteen on the ship, because when palletisation come in and the fork-lift came in the dock, the eight men went to three..that's when the severance pay came in. And then the thirteen men in the gang went down to seven, because you only had two men down the hatch."

The dockers and stevedores became notorious during the 1960s and 1970s for their union militancy and wild-cat or unofficial strikes and stoppages. Their behaviour, widely criticised by the media, did not endear them to the general public, nor to the port authority, nor to the shipping lines using the port. Behind their militant action lay the years of low pay and insecurity, the desire to share some of the benefits of the post-war boom in the port and the need to protect their livelihoods. In the 1950s, men still competed for work "on the stones", as George Adams wrote: "...when work was scarce the floaters (not attached to a regular gang) would mob that part of the stones where fresh work was being called; some would tarry and then plonk themselves in front of the crowd..others who were pressed back by the crush would stand on tip-toe or scamper along to a thinner part of the crowd."

Another port worker remembered from the 1950s and 1960s that "..even the flies would not go near our toilets", and described the filthy working conditions and lack of facilities. The docks were plagued with rats. A young man going to work as a sampler in the Millwall Docks in the 1950s recalled: "the scampering of tiny feet as scores of rats and mice scurried across the floor to their bolt holes when the lights were switched on". Where cattle skins (a source of the deadly anthrax) were being handled, there would be: "...photos of skin sores on the dock wall as a warning and a bucket of diluted disinfectant on deck and a bit of cotton waste to wipe yourself; you had to be quick or someone would wash their boots in it. When the set used to go over your head with the wet skins that used to drip on you..." Dirty and dusty cargoes, such as graphite, cement or pulverised bones, meant travelling home filthy, and the dust of the bones created hard lumps, "like little stones" in the nostrils; graphite stuck to the skin: "..no matter how hard you washed – dreadful stuff! You had to clean your eyes with Vaseline." But: "...you couldn't pick and choose. Most men were happy to get the work."

It became increasingly clear in the late 1960s and early 1970s that job losses in the up-river docks were going to run into tens of thousands; that modernisation was coming "too little and too late"; and that strikes and stoppages would not prevent the decline. Over time, difficult negotiations achieved an ending of the casual system in London's docks, replaced by a registration scheme with a guaranteed wage for every worker. Piece work was replaced by shifts and severance schemes were introduced.

"Decasualisation" could be costly for the stevedoring firms, such as Scrutton's and Maltby's, who supplied the port with labour to load ships and who had been accustomed to paying only for the labour they needed. One ex-stevedore explained how he preferred the casual system: "...I didn't mind at the time, because you got a blow from work, though you never had the money, and when you came back you worked hard and earned the money". As soon as the stevedoring companies had to retain a full labour force: "...a lot of them went bust...because they had to pay these men a high upstanding rate and not be able to put them back on the pool and use their labour as they wanted to use it."

The ending of piece work was seen by some as another factor in the decline of the docks. "...I think that was the greatest thing ever, to have piece work, and that incentive to work. Terrific. I mean, when they took that out of the dock it completely ruined it...How could you pay people who were not doing anything, I mean, it's crazy, isn't it? I mean, people were just coming to work and there was no work for them."

Circumstances like this contributed to the popular image of "dockers" (the media and general public did not distinguish between the different grades of workers) as lazy, idle and good-for-nothing,

which was fiercely resented. "That was rubbish, absolute rubbish. I have come out of a ship's hull at half past four in the morning and that is from quarter to eight in the morning, you had to be there...".

But in time-honoured tradition, older men looked upon young workers as having it too easy:

1961, discharging logs into lighter from a vessel at the West India Docks. John Vagg on the left, and George Pratt on the right.

"...They did work hard in those days to what they do today (1979). My husband come out of the dock in 1967, he said then, all they wanted to know was a comb to comb their quiff and a watch on their arm to see if they were missing out on time; he said they never worked as hard as he did." (Dot Bennett)

The dock workers of the late 1960s could shelter from bad weather in amenity blocks where there were showers and lockers. Towards the end they were issued with protective clothing, including boots and different gloves for different cargoes.

By the time there was only one shipping company left in the Millwall Docks, conditions had improved beyond the wildest dreams of the pre-war port workers: "...we moved to Olsen's then, because that is all that was left in the docks. Terrific, down there. Social club. We had a marvellous canteen there. Breakfast in the morning. When you was on the late shift you had dinner in the morning at five o'clock...subsidised. Social, Saturday evening. All the crowd would get round there of a Saturday night. Pension scheme. Marvellous. It was great. I had seven years there. Out of all my time I would say that was the best years of my life." (George Pye)

A complex set of circumstances led to the closure of the up-river docks. Insufficient investment in modernising the system was one; the cost of labour and redundancy another; the threat of strikes played a part in the decline in business, but world trade was dropping in the 1970s and with less business to go round, the cheaper rates offered to shipping by modern ports like Felixstowe and Ipswich was just as significant.

These circumstances also applied to the wharves which ran all round the edge of the Isle of Dogs and lined both banks of the Thames into the heart of the City. Some wharves belonged to a company, such as C. & E. Mortons, or Associated Lead. Others were wharfage companies operating in their own right as import, storage and transport services, such as Winkley's Wharf and Cook's Wharf. Many riverside wharves were equipped with old warehouses and out-dated hydraulic machinery and were unsuitable for modern handling equipment, whilst road access, designed for horses and carts, was often too narrow for lorries. Cook's Wharf in Manchester Road had 4,700,000 cubic feet of storage space, including bonded warehouses where goods were stored prior to duty being paid. Commodities handled there included grains, spices, dried fruits, coffee beans, cocoa beans and rubber. In 1958 the controlling interest in Cooks was acquired by William Cory & Son Ltd., a public company with a variety of interests both on and off the river. Activity on the wharf gradually declined with the fall in river traffic and relocation of storage.

Wharves attached to manufacturing companies also fell into disuse as they turned instead to the convenience of motor transport. However, some wharfage companies were able to adapt to a certain extent until circumstances combined to force most of the up-river wharves out of business in the 1970s, with compensation paid to the redundant dockers, as this former crane driver recounts:

"My mate who was also a docker, a wharf-side docker, told me they needed a crane driver down Winkley's Wharf, which is up at the Kingsbridge. I went to see the governor there and he said he'd like to have me if I could get transferred down there. Anyway I ended up down Winkley's Wharf, driving a crane and it was very good down there. It was about thirty men, all craft work down there, no ships, and I was driving the crane all day long, which wasn't too bad. So I was quite happy. Then Winkley's Wharf folded. And I was choked about that. I'd only been there about 20 months when it folded and every man got the same whether he'd been there twenty years or not and I ended up with eighteen hundred compensation there." (Bill S.)

The crane-driver was assigned to work in Tilbury Docks where he remained until 1980. Then he became a caretaker, then a black cab driver.

This one story is typical of thousands, as the port workforce dwindled and dispersed and the river and docks below Tower Bridge lost the noise and bustle

June 1980, stevedores from Millwall and West India Docks in the Dock Staff and Labour Club having a last drink together before the docks closed.

they had known since the Middle Ages. With it all went a way of working, full of hardship, but with its own special quality, as remembered here:

"The old ones, well, they done their quota, a lot of them was good old workers, really good workers... they would be there all day, work, work, work... I was working with blokes that was 65, 68, and could still do a day's work... As long as they was working, we didn't mind. Because they was interesting, wasn't they? I mean, they are old characters, I mean, it used to be enjoyable to go to work and hear them talk, it was great, really great. Looking back over it, I really miss it, I really do. I mean, they had arguments and fights and laughs and God, it was unbelievable!" (George A.)

As the docks and wharves closed, so did the ship repair yards and the barge-building yards. As fewer ships came up the river, there was less work in the dry-docks which lined the Thames. Fewer barges were needed to transport cargoes from ship to store and so the barge-yards too closed down. Here too, the loss of the companionship of the workplace was keenly felt, as former barge-builder John Penn recalled in 1984:

"I left school when I was 14 years old and I went into a barge yard. It was a bad winter, in 1944. I was made an apprentice, a seven-year apprentice. In those days, your mother or your father took you down to the yard and had a chat with the governor and he said, "We'll look after him," and all this sort of business and your father had to sign your apprenticeship papers. So then I'm allowed into the barge yard.

I had to learn how to use my tools. We was given a set of tools, that was a few chisels, a mallet, two wooden planes, an adze, a flogger, and we had to look after them, we had to oil them up and grease them up and the barge builders taught us how to use them and we became very good with our tools, you know, with the adze we became very good, we always took pride, especially in the adze, taking thin slices, then thinner, paper thin, you know, which was very hard to do...

...Then it started to get really bad, the river started to decline a lot. And so I thought, it's not going to last much longer, the way we're going, now I'd started at 14 years old and I'd worked right through my life on the river and I thought, well, I'll see if I can change and I went into the building business and I could never get on with that, that wasn't my cup of tea,

When you worked in a barge yard like Bay Wharf Construction Company and Union Lighterage, in those early days, it was like a family concern, you know, you used to go in and everybody was your brother, you used to skylark around with everybody. You knew and you got to love your mates, sort of thing, you treated them well and they treated you well and it was very rarely you had any arguments in a yard like that and I worked there fifteen year. Yeah, and you

Tony Elsley, Cecil Fitzearle, John Penn and Ray Fitzearle, in the garden of a prefab in Plevna Street, 1954.

were so knitted together in those times that you can't really describe it, you had a couple of arguments, but nothing, you used to talk to everybody, everybody used to have a laugh, you used to call out and have a joke with anybody you passed in your yard, and remember you're talking about 150 men, you knew everybody by their name, you knew all their personal troubles, you were so knitted together in a yard like that, it was marvellous and that's why when I went out in the building trade you could see one man one day and he was gone the next. See one man one day, gone the next...there wasn't the closeness of relationships, there wasn't that closeness. One day you'd see a bloke and the next day he'd be gone, and you couldn't leave your tools laying anywhere because they'd be pinched.

I came back into the shipping but eventually it just died, the barge yards went. Hughams packed up, Pipers are going, just across the river, Union Lighterage packed up, Bay Wharf Construction packed up, they've all declined, they've gone. They don't build them now, there's no use for them, they've got so many barges now they don't know what to do with them, they're burning them up, some of them docks down there are full up of them, they don't know what to do with them."

John Penn also described how he saw changing methods in barge building lead to job losses. "...when they got the welded barge, so it was, Just run a weld along there. Done away with the caulker, done away with the riveter, done away with the holder-upper, done away with the forgeman, so there was jobs galore lost there."

For several years before he finally retired, John Penn worked at the Museum of Docklands restoring river barges and other artefacts.

Bob Strudwick worked at steel erectors Westwood's, in the 1950s and 1960s, and he too valued the companionship of his workmates:

"The company had two sites. The main works was on the river side of Westferry Road and was entered under an arch, with the gatehouse and weighbridge control on the right. The much smaller sheet metal works was on the opposite side of this road. The large site included stores, offices, parking areas and three or four fabrication shops. Each of these was an open portal framed structure, about 60 feet wide and 450 feet long. The two outer shops had sheeting on the outside face as weather protection. Each shop had two overhead travelling cranes lifting about five tons each. The crane driver sat in a cabin hung beneath the crane and moved along the shop whenever somebody wanted assistance – by calling "Crane!" The heating in the shops was by coke fires and they gave off very distinct fumes.

There were three grades of draughtsmen – senior, intermediate and junior. There were also three estimators, a typist and a printer, Shirley Smith. She printed all the company drawings with an arc-lamp dyeline printer. As office junior I would answer phones, help with the printing, run errands in the works and visit the local shops twice each day to keep the office supplied with sweets and cigarettes. In between, I would be tracing old drawings to develop my hand-printing and drawing skills. As my skills developed I prepared fabrication drawings and assisted in site surveys. I attended Technical College under the Day Release Scheme.

I left Westwood's to earn more money in the oil industry. My time there was the best job I ever had and this was due in large part to the people I worked with."

Young people who showed promise, especially boys, were very often encouraged to learn under various apprenticeship and day-release schemes. Harry Jenkins' grandson, who, like Harry's sons, worked for Montague Meyer's, was sent to different parts of the country to learn aspects of the timber trade and was also helped through college by the firm. He went on to have his own business.

Westwood's closed in the 1970s. Steel erectors Matthew T.Shaw in Westferry Road was another victim of change in the 1970s, when there was a fall in demand for their products. In spite of an attempt to start a sideline in canal cruisers, the company went into liquidation and the works was closed down and sold off.

In the yard of J.Westwood & Co., Westferry Road, repairing the cutting shield used in the Dartford Tunnel, for use in the construction of the new Blackwall Tunnel. The white deposit on the base is chalk from the first tunnelling.

Other Island firms were disappearing, for various reasons. George Clark's sugar refining works in Alpha Road felt the pinch of ever-fiercer competition as by the early 1950s the number of their customers, the breweries, had shrunk to only 300. Peter Trafford Clark, director and a descendant of the founder, took the company in new directions which involved heavy investment in plant, diversifying into the production of caramels for the food and drinks industries, golden syrup for stores such as Sainsbury's and speciality syrups for Europe. Success brought the firm into direct

Loading bulk liquid sugar at George Clark's refinery, Alpha Road (later Tate & Lyle).

Montague Meyer's, timber importers, works' team, 1948-1950. In back row: W.Garland, Alf Sibthorpe, Bill James, Bert Lander, Wally Gibson. Middle row, J.Fry, Sid Harris, Bill Gilbert. Front: E.Prudence, Joe Walsham, - Caldis, J.Ayres and P.Tully.

competition with larger and more powerful organisations. In the late 1950s a take-over bid from United States giant Corn Products Company through their UK operation, Brown and Poulson, proved irresistible to Clark's shareholders and the Broadway Works in Alpha Road ceased to be a family business. By 1964, output was 33,000 tons per year with a staff of 150; most of this was in liquid sugar and liquid glucose for confectionery and soft drinks manu-facturers, delivered in bulk tankers. In that year

Daisy Roberts and Dolly Morris taking a tea break at Hawkins & Tipson's rope works, in 1954. The sharp knife attached to string round Daisy's waist was made in the works, and was used to cut rope quickly if it began to kink or if anything else went wrong on the machine; fingers and thumbs could be lost through a moment's carelessness.

Workers from McDougall's Flour Mill on an outing to Southend in 1948.

"Millwall Sugars" was bought by Tate & Lyle. Redundancies and increased mechanisation followed, with output rising to 41,000 tons with 85 employees. The Millwall branch of Tate & Lyle was one of the few Island industries to survive into the twenty-first century.

Experiments with rope made from nylon and

In the yard of Klondyke Garage, Westferry Road, opposite the old Maconochie's factory; one of the men is Bernard Silcock.

other artificial fibres were given a boost by the needs of wartime and in 1946 the manufacture of synthetic rope began at the Hawkins and Tipson ropeworks. Nylon rope did not prove popular with ship and tug owners and in 1961 Imperial Chemical Industries (I.C.I.) produced their first Terylene fibre rope which stretched evenly and was much more useful as marine rope. This was developed at the Millwall factory in co-operation with I.C.I. and among the first users were Esso Petroleum's 60,000 ton tankers.

In 1964, in response to the threat of competition, Hawkins & Tipson set up their own Trinidad Ropeworks at Arima, 40 miles outside Port of Spain, using surplus equipment and machinery shipped out from the Millwall plant. The top Millwall ropemaker, Bill Power, who had just lost his wife, went out to Trinidad to train a team of ropemakers there and commence manufacture.

By 1971 the Millwall factory had become outdated and the site was too restricted to be adapted to modern handling methods. Millwall production was transferred to Hailsham in Sussex; a few key members of staff went along, but most of the Island ropemakers became redundant. Hawkins & Tipsons built themselves a new office/warehouse at Thamesmead, which was opened by Prime Minister Edward Heath in October 1971.

McDougalls employed dozens of local men and women in handling, grading and packing at the flour mill beside Millwall Dock; they also had laboratories on the premises for analysis and quality control. In

1962 the firm celebrated its centenary with a grand dinner dance in the centre of London, when all the workers were transported in a fleet of coaches. "Happy times" one office worker recalled.

For the Island's transport and haulage firms, change was rapid in the post-war years. After surviving the Second World War, the Huish family company was nationalised in 1949 and taken over by British Road Services. Five years passed with difficulty, then in 1954: "We started to buy back the licences and a very costly business this proved to be – each vehicle bought was almost scrap and had to be rebuilt or replaced.....nevertheless we continued in business and for many years we expanded steadily. In 1963 we had to move from our Island premises under a compulsory order. We were allocated a bomb-site in Poplar and work began on a new depot. Then, almost overnight, the whole tempo of work changed....having to move containers which arrived from Sweden and weighed anything from ten to twenty tons. At this time, we and many other hauliers had no suitable vehicles to perform this work. But we survived again, until in 1972 the principal customer closed the shipping business and we were forced to curtail our operations."

Davison's family firm in Westferry Road also survived the war by about 20 years, growing from being transport contractors to a conglomerate involving transport, fuel oils and storage. They sold up to the Transport Development Group when one of the partners, George Davison, decided to retire following an illness.

In 1943 the giant colour firm, Burrell's, sold its paint-making trade to Hamers of Mitcham and went on to concentrate on colour and chemical manufacture, supplying the print, dye, paint-making, motor car and plastics industries. By the 1970s the firm had a new headquarters in the Broadway, Stratford, and five separate factories – two on Millwall, one in Derbyshire, one in Cheshire and one in Stratford, with export sales to the United States, Africa, Australia and Europe.

In the early 1970s the *Island Contact* magazine reported the closure of Stephens Smith & Co., London Yard, suppliers of machinery and tanks to the food and medical equipment industries; and of Badcocks, barge builders and repairers, also on London Yard, and commented: "this is not the first firm that has closed down and the story is the same for each...a combination of failing trade, inaccessibility of the factory, difficulty of finding staff, site too small..."

As unemployment and redundancy bit harder in the late 1970s, Islanders, adaptable as ever, turned to the service, shopping and the leisure industries – buying and selling, mini-cab or black cab driving, cleaning and caretaking. Some invested their redundancy money in opening a shop or running a

Ready for the annual outing, workers at Beecham's factory, formerly C & E Morton's, including Louie Neal, Helen Noding, Violet Neal, Margaret Evans, Mary Blackall, Charlie Stock, Ivy Isitt, Sam Searle, Harry Warren, Peter Clack, Sylvia Haben, Betty Marsh, Flo Burgess, Mrs Stock (in top hat), Flo Marney, Jessie Stock, Lil Nichols and Frank Crossley.

pub; others found a new role in community projects, or in one of the local government agencies, or settled into early retirement with their grandchildren, pigeons, bingo club, allotments and bowls. More and more of the young unemployed had to look further afield for work, into the great bustle of the capital with its abundant opportunities. Between the wars, 75% of Islanders had worked locally. By the 1970s, the figures were reversed, and 70% of those in work, worked away.

Hand-in-hand with the run-down of the docks went the plans for the redevelopment of the entire area from the Tower to Beckton or "Docklands" as it now began to be known. In 1971 the London Docklands Study Team was set up by the Heath government, with consultants Travers Morgan commissioned to come up with a comprehensive redevelopment plan. The Travers Morgan Report, published in 1973, proposed to develop the area with golf courses, water sports and private housing. In response, opposition groups united to form the Joint Docklands Action Group (JDAG), representing the view that the area should be redeveloped, in consultation with local people, to make use of existing skills and resources. "Homes before Hotels" and "People Before Profits" said the posters outside the opening ceremony of the Tower Hotel at St.Katherine's Dock. The contrast between the poverty and deprivation experienced by people already living in Docklands, and the millions of pounds invested in private development, was to be a recurring theme over the decades which followed.

The Travers Morgan Report was abandoned and

under the Labour Government which was elected in 1973 the Docklands Joint Committee was set up, representing the GLC and five London Boroughs, with responsibility to oversee the development of the area. In 1976, after a lengthy consultation process, the DJC produced the London Docklands Strategic Plan (LDSP). This outlined a future based on employment suited to the skills of existing residents in Docklands, with substantial public sector funding as well as private investment, to: "redress the housing, social, environmental, employment, economic and communications deficiencies of the Docklands area".

For several reasons, this optimistic plan could not work. It was criticised for focussing too closely on local interests and what is more, there was no practical way in which the DJC could carry out all its proposals, since it did not own the land, and the whole structure of the Committee, representing five boroughs and the GLC, was too complex for effective decision-making. Some proposals, like the Southern Relief Road, which threatened to cut the Island in two, were dropped in the face of opposition. Others were implemented, including the relocation of Billingsgate Fish Market to the West India Docks, and the construction of small business units at Canon Workshops.

As the Docklands Joint Committee struggled to meet its targets, events were overtaking the planners and council officers. Firms were closing down and people were leaving the area. Remaining residents and business owners were frustrated at the continued lack of action after so many years of proposals and promises. When the Conservatives came to power in

1983: South Quay, West India Docks, Blue Bridge in distance. The Isle of Dogs anglers enjoying the leisure of unemployment, fishing in the unused waters of the docks.

1979, and turned their attention to London Docklands, they found that there was little to show for the years of planning. Michael Heseltine, Secretary of State for the Environment, decided that power should be given to a single agency, which would take the decisions which the local boroughs had not been able to agree on.

The Local Government Land and Planning Act of 1980 created the London Docklands Development Corporation (LDDC) charged with regenerating the area. This was to be done by improving roads and other services and by clearing sites for development, thus attracting private investment. The work was to be paid for with public funds and income from the sale of land. As a further incentive to speculative building, an Enterprise Zone was created on the Isle of Dogs, where there were minimum planning controls, tax concessions and a ten-year period free of rates. The LDDC was not elected, it was not answerable to the general public or the local authorities, although it was intended to work with them, and it had no brief for addressing social issues such as housing and education.

The stage was now set for a transformation of local employment. In the next twenty years, the decline in trade and manufacturing would continue until these traditional types of work had all but disappeared; instead, three new areas of work would become dominant: financial and business agencies; distribution, hotels and catering; and printing and publishing.

9. Homes and Family Life

During the Second World War, a large proportion of the Island's housing stock was damaged or destroyed. Even though the population had fallen to less than half its pre-war numbers, there was a chronic shortage of decent housing in the post-war years. The task of rebuilding was taken on by the local authorities and it was a slow process, not completed until the 1970s. By this time the population had risen to around 15,000 with the addition of new residents from other areas of London. Meanwhile, living standards had improved, thanks to the new health and welfare services, the post-war economic boom and cheap consumer goods. Family life was also changing with a rise in divorce and single parents, and the decline of the close extended family.

ARP Warden Dave Marsden recorded in his war-time diary: "Anyone who had been familiar with the district and had been away for three months would have been staggered at the amount of damage done, for there are whole streets turned into heaps of rubble and on the heaps of what were houses one can see parts of every kind of furniture sticking out... pictures still hanging precariously...a child's cot in light green and the bedroom door sliding to the bottom..."

Whole families had packed up and left. The experience of Billy O'Neill's family from Westferry Road was typical. They had relatives and friends living in the new estates built in the 1930s in Dagenham and Becontree. They moved in with them and were eventually rehoused and settled down there:

"...us four, along with Nanny O'Neill, who was nearly ninety, stayed with Aunt Liz and Uncle Bill Johnson in Marlborough Road. Aunt Bridget and Uncle Frank with Paddy stayed with Fred and Nell Marsh in Babington Road, Aunt Florrie and Uncle Jack Avis along with Bill, daughter Florrie and her husband Harry Hatt stayed with family friends in Gorsebrook Road, Dagenham. The Anderson shelter in the back garden of Marlborough Road then became our home for six months, until we got rehoused in Parkway. We lived there until April 1941, until we got bombed out again, eventually finishing up in Boreham Wood to stay with Nanny Marsh and linking up my mother's sisters again. Aunt Bridget eventually got her own home in Babington Road and finished her days there, Aunt Florrie and family were housed in Oval Road North in Dagenham before moving back to the Island to Hubert House in Janet Street where she died."

Newly-weds Elsie and George Jamieson moved house several times because of the war: "George and I lived in Greenwich for six weeks. After Greenwich we moved to Overcliff Road, Lewisham, it was there we were bombed out by a "Buzz Bomb" on 27th June 1944 and lost most of our home. George had been called up for the Navy in 1943 as they needed shipwrights out in the Far East. After the war we were given a temporary home at Catford, didn't like it there, then in 1946 we were moved into the prefabs at Lewisham built on the site where we had lost our home. After 1952 we were offered a house at Grove Park where we remained."

In this way Island neighbourhoods were broken up as people moved and moved again, scattered like leaves in the wind, and the eastward movement of Islanders and other Londoners, which had been noticeable in the 1920s and 1930s, continued. Alf French was "amazed" when he later lived in Manor Park, and got to know Ilford: "...the enormous number of people living there who had lived in the East End, or their parents had."

For some people, moving out to Essex was not ideal. Mrs Logan had been living in Glen Terrace with her mother: "I was rehoused from the LCC I think it was, but they housed me out at Harold Wood... it was a brand new estate and there was no transport, there was nothing, so my husband used to have to walk from Harold Wood right in to Romford before he could get any transport to get to work. He was a crane driver, worked on Canning Town Bridge and he used to get fed up with this walk, walk, walk, 'cos he used to have to get in early to light the crane up and get things ready, so he said, Ask you mother if we can

Community life continues after the war amongst old neighbours who have moved to Dagenham. Here members of Island families the Churches and the Blackburns celebrate the 1953 Coronation with a traditional street party.

have our two rooms back. I think she missed us as much as we missed her so I went back there…"

People made homeless by bombing and who wanted to stay on the Island moved around from cellars, to shelters, to houses abandoned by others. Rose Marsh recalled:

"Next door to the Ivy House in Manchester Road was Number 334, the last house I lived in before the last-but-one rocket, or doodlebug, I'm not sure which, fell on the Rye Arc Welding works, making us homeless. We were asleep at the time. I believe the reason we were living at Number 334 was that we had been bombed out of our own house, and people just used to go and live in any vacant houses where families had gone away or been evacuated. After that we had to live in Glengall Road School for some weeks, until the prefabs were built in 1945 to rehouse the homeless families. My Mum had to go to a Welfare Centre in Bow to get some furniture to put in our prefab when we were allocated one in Plevna Street. When I got married I moved to the Canada Estate in Preston's Road, Ontario House. After a few years I moved back to a vacant prefab next-door-but-one to Mum, where I stayed until they moved us out for redevelopment in 1963."

Prefabricated homes were designed to deal with the crisis in housing. The very first "Box bungalows" or "hut-homes" built of asbestos and wood with steel window frames, were installed on the Island in Glengall Grove in September 1944. Designed to be erected in a few days and to be used for a maximum

of two years, each new temporary home had a living room with a dining recess and kitchenette, and two bedrooms. They were built on cleared bomb sites where water, electricity, gas and mains drainage were already laid on or near at hand. There were no inside toilets, but outside closets built in blocks of four.

Mrs Green, one of the first tenants, said: "…think what it means to have an electric cooker and to have them all round the table for proper meals; to have a nice clean sink and good food cupboards and decent beds – this is wonderful!" However the huts proved to be damp and cold, and in 1948 a group of the tenants lobbied Parliament, detailing the illnesses which had affected every family living in the huts.

The "Portal" homes were an improvement on the first prefabs. Designed to last for ten years, they had asbestos walls on a steel frame, plaster-board partitions, three bedrooms and inside bathrooms. 300 of these were erected in Cubitt Town. The "prefabs" as they soon came to be known, lasted much longer than ten years in some cases, and have been recalled with affection: "We were in the prefab for nineteen years. They were new – they were lovely! I'd like to have stopped in them. The kitchenette was small, but we had a fridge, we had built-in wardrobes, nice-sized rooms and it was all on the level. We had a garden – that was the main thing! We had a bathroom and inside toilet which we never had before. We had a fire with a back boiler for hot water. Everybody liked them. I miss the old prefab." (Mrs Warren)

The "prefabs" were only a stop-gap, and new

house-building had to begin. On a national scale the situation was worse if anything than after the First World War. The inter-war slum clearance programme had never been completed. During six years of war, house-building had been at a standstill whilst hundreds of thousands of homes had been destroyed or damaged. In the same period, two million marriages had taken place and the birth rate was rising.

On the Island, where over 1,000 homes were destroyed and many surviving houses were badly damaged, the *Church Times* in 1947 described : "...old brick houses, many bearing the marks of battering in the raids, all grimy with factory smoke". These old homes were densely overcrowded, the article went on, especially in the houses where a young man demobilised from the Army had returned and settled with his wife and children in the parents' home. One house with three bedrooms had in it a married daughter with her husband and baby, the

Mrs Maud Green and John Green, in 1932. John Green was a maintenance engineer who worked at East Ferry Engineering, Woolwich Arsenal, Morton's and Montague Meyer's. Mrs Green worked in the offices of various Island firms and was well-known as a pianist in local pubs. They had one of the first prefabs.

grandparents, and four girls and four boys aged from seven to twenty.

All sorts of solutions had to be adopted by newly-weds in search of a home. One couple slept in the corridor of the family pre-fab until they found a room to rent. Elsie Callen, who worked in McDougalls, married her stevedore husband in May 1947. They had nowhere to live:

"We had a quiet wedding with only close family and a few friends. In the evening we went to see a show, *Perchance to Dream*. A house or even rooms to rent then were very hard to get, so we decided to live apart, hoping that something would turn up for us. The furniture we bought was put in store. Sure enough, two months later, a distant relative had three rooms available for us to rent and we moved in straight away. The house was in Deptford and meant it took longer to travel to work, but we didn't mind – we had a place of our own."

One of the priorities of the post-war Labour Government was to subsidise new house-building by the local authorities. For Londoners, this was to include the two new towns of Basildon and Harlow which were to house 300,000 people, in addition to new housing estates at Harold Hill and Becontree.

With the housing stock reduced by approximately 50% during the war, Poplar Borough Council still had 5,000 applicants on its housing register in 1948. The severe winter of 1947 and the shortage of materials in the post-war austerity years had slowed down the building programme. On the Island, progress seemed painfully slow. In the bomb-damaged houses in Manchester Road and elsewhere, the leaking roofs, blocked drains and lack of amenities seemed as bad as they had been after the First World War. In May 1951 the occupants of some of these old houses said Poplar Labour councillors were "getting complacent" and challenged them to an open debate about housing on the Isle of Dogs. Publicity about the building programme had raised expectations, which were not being fulfilled.

In the 1950s permanent building by the local authorities at last got underway again on the Island They bought up acres of privately owned land, pulled down what remained of the old Victorian streets and erected houses and blocks of maisonettes. New designs and materials were tried out, like the breeze-block "Orlit" houses, and in 1951, the Festival of Britain year, the Lansbury Estate round Chrisp Street market was promoted as the way forward for working-class housing. Most people wanted houses with gardens, but architects and planners had to consider the greater number of homes which could be provided with the available land and money. In the 1950s and 1960s blocks of flats and maisonettes were considered the best solution. In 1955 additional subsidies were provided for blocks over six storeys high and in the same year the Isle of Dogs Housing Society built a block of 55 dwellings, in Pier Street, named Betty

May Gray House after a benefactress who had made a large donation to the Society.

In the early 1960s there was public anger at a slow-down in council house building which increased dependence on private landlords. Privately-owned property still existed here and there on the Island and while controlled rents were cheap, uncontrolled rents were not. Rising land values, and the high interest rates which municipal authorities had to pay on their loans for building, had raised the cost of building a council house from £2,500 to between £4,000 and £6000. This was reflected in rising rents.

This was at a time when speculative building was beginning to create empty office space in many areas. In 1962, at a meeting called by Millwall Residents' Association in Cubitt Town Library, attended by tenants and residents from all over East London, it was agreed that the following resolution be sent to the local authorities: "Offices or similar properties that are not occupied within six months should be requisitioned to provide homes for at least five years." In 1964 the *East London Advertiser* reported overcrowding in Harbinger Road and Hesperus Crescent. A couple and their two children were living in one room in their parents' house, another baby was expected and they had been promised a home in 1966 at the earliest. These kinds of pressure led to the drastic solution of tower blocks. The Samuda Estate, with its multi-storey Kelson House, and the Barkantine with its four tower blocks, are classic examples of the housing policy of the mid-sixties.

St.John's Estate (named after the old church) was built on the Island between 1963 and 1966, providing homes in low rise dwellings grouped around enclosed greens which were private to the families living there. There were gardens and balconies, warm air heating, fitted cupboards, and a public open space to serve the area. This included two tennis courts, a putting course, two football pitches and a netball court, as well as a play area for small children. In 1968 the estate won a commendation for its good design from the Civic Trust. Adjacent to St.John's Estate is Castalia Square, where shops and maisonettes were built in the 1960s. Estates around Christ Church followed in the early 1970s and by 1975, 95% of Island homes were provided by the local authorities,

The Greater London Council was created in 1965, at the same time as Tower Hamlets Borough Council. Under the GLC, housing was allocated according to need on a London-wide basis, and this resulted in many people being uprooted from their home neighbourhoods and relocated somewhere else. The population was shifting and changing as Islanders settled in other places and new people came to the Island.

Pockets of sub-standard housing remained. Flats in Westferry Estate which still had shared bathrooms, or had a bath in the kitchen, were modernised in the late 1960s. In the mid-1970s women living in the Canada Estate in Prestons Road wrote to the Prime Minister, Margaret Thatcher, about the overflowing drains, vermin and atrocious conditions in which they were living. The estate lay in the path of the proposed New Southern Relief Road and plans for its demolition had prevented any maintenance work being done. The last tenants were moved out in November 1979.

**No.88 Manchester Road,
prior to demolition in the 1970s.**

In the new post-war housing, living conditions were generally an improvement on pre-war standards. People earned higher wages and more consumer goods had come on the market. Expectations were higher. The slogan "Live now, pay later" took hold. Credit became easier and hire purchase firms, an extension of the old "tally man", flourished, allowing people to buy fitted carpets and new furniture..

Rising real wages made a noticeable difference very soon after the war. In 1949 St.Mildred's Settlement *Annual Report* noted: "Gone are the days when we distributed large joints of meat at Christmas. Gone too are the days when children were genuinely pleased to receive second-hand toys and books. We must be thankful...because it means that standards of living have improved."

In 1953 St.Mildred's *Report* said: "...incomes can vary by hundreds of pounds per year for the same size of family....only a tiny minority of our neighbours put anything aside as savings... We have neighbours who own a television set, a motor-bicycle and side-car, maybe even a car (which they keep parked in their open street all the year round) and bicycles for the

Top picture opposite: St.John's Estate in 1958, prefabs in Galbraith Street in the foreground.

Lower picture opposite: Manchester Road and the Samuda Estate being built, 1968. Stephen and Karen Sime are the children, they lived at No.399.

8 Kingfield Street, home of the Price family, with Eunice Pratt and Tony Fedden, both students at the old George Green School; and Joan Price, a clerk at Barclays Bank. The TV is a nine-inch black and white.

1960, Daisy and Thomas Clayden on the Isle of Wight: "We went twice, once that year, because he had won some money and we decided to spend it on a holiday; the second time was when he retired and we had a fortnight then."

children. Some go on expensive holidays for their fortnight off work during the year. A great deal is spent on children... new outfits, all to match, for Christmas..huge dolls and dolls' prams and other expensive toys... all the luxuries of the home are bought on the Hire Purchase system. everything is paid for in weekly instalments, even the bedding and the children's clothes."

A Hire Purchase card from Thompson's of Salmon Lane, dated 1954, for two pairs of blankets, revealed that the total cost was twelve pounds eighteen shillings and ten pence, deposit one pound, weekly payments two shillings and sixpence.

Not everyone was better-off; poverty persisted.

The work of the Children's Country Holiday Fund was still needed, and there were plenty of school children who qualified under the 1944 Education Act for free meals and help with buying clothes.

In the early 1960s Timewell's Travel Agency was advertising trips to "anywhere in the UK" and "Continental Coach Touring Holidays with Sea, Rail or Air Travel" They were also "Agents for Butlins Camps and Hotels". Harry Neave, of Chrisp Street, sold "Washing Machines and Refrigerators" and British Relay Wireless Limited of Bow Road were advertising British Relay TV as "the television of the future" with "push-button choice of radio and TV".

The older generation were more cautious about the new wealth than their children.

"It was not until my Father had retired from the Docks that they were able to afford holidays and that was only as far as Guernsey where they stayed with relatives. My parents never owned their own home or car, and even rented a television for fear of not being able to afford repairs. (Kit Bragger, nee Bruce)

"We bought our first TV in 1949. Black and white, of course. We invited Mum and Dad to see the first programme and they were thrilled. Later on when we were able to afford one, we bought a small car and took them to Margate for the day. They thought it was wonderful." (Mrs Winnett, nee Peacock)

In the new Island housing estates tenants were learning the rules laid down by the local authority. They were advised that:

"Carpets must be beaten or shaken before 10 o'clock in the morning...no walls may be papered or painted without the consent of the appropriate committee". Trying to exercise control over traditional activities, the council explained that no garden shed could be erected without permission, adding that permission might be granted to keep a limited number of poultry. The same *Municipal Tenants Handbook* advised tenants to keep food in the larder, "where it is cooler" (refrigerators were still relatively rare); how to unblock drains; how to deal with rats, cockroaches, crickets, fleas and wild pigeons and how to avoid bed bugs, which "may arrive with an article of second-hand furniture." There was a section on "The Electrical Installation in Your Home"; this included drying cabinets and immersion heaters, a blessing (at a cost) to families accustomed to the old kitchen range or copper as their only source of heat and hot water.

But in the old housing conditions remained much the same as in pre-war years Looking back to the 1960s, Pat Jones remembered: "We had an outside toilet...an old tin bath in front of the fire every Friday night...The scullery was so small, all that was in it was an old gas oven, a great big enamel sink with only cold

Opposite: Reg Rayner, of Cubitt Town with his grand-daughter Susan in her christening robe, 1971.

running water and a beaten up cupboard with a wonky work surface that Mum dished up the dinner on...in the best room was an old two-seater settee and a large mat covering the lino. My Mum was so houseproud even though the house was falling down around us. I can still picture her cleaning the windows, lifting the window up and sitting on the ledge, spending more time chatting to the passers-by than getting the job done. I can see her polishing our doorstep and cleaning the door handle with Brasso

Mrs Martha Fitzearle in the garden of her Plevna Street prefab, 1953. The mangle came with the family from 338 Manchester Road, where they were bombed out.

once a week. We never had fitted carpets, My Mum always cleaned the lino with a dustpan and brush – What was a Hoover?"

It was impossible to "chat to the neighbours" whilst cleaning the windows on the 10th floor of a tower block and the new living quarters played a part in making people feel isolated, although family life was changing in other ways too. There were still some big families, but generally family size was declining with rising living standards and with the advent of health and welfare clinics advising on effective birth control. Family networks of several generations had been broken up by the war and though some survived, new ones were not easily created, or desired, now that modern housing conditions and better welfare

provisions made people less dependent on each other. Divorce rates were rising and the nuclear family itself was less stable than it had been.

St. Mildred's commented in 1951 that: "There are, alas, very many homes where there are matrimonial troubles between parents and we are asked to try to help unhappiness and instability in the children." In 1952 they noted the increase in the number of working mothers, particularly since the "twilight shift" had become common. It was now very difficult to find a few moments at home with the mother of a family for a quiet talk: "She is out at work all day. The children have dinner at school, they have their own latch key at an early age and access to matches and the stove to get their own tea. They are at a loose end in the dinner hour and after school and often get into trouble. When mother comes in she has to set to and clean the house, or maybe she is too tired to do much and sits in a chair beside father and watches the television whose weekly hire-purchase payments she is helping him to keep up by going to work herself."

But in fairness the Report went on: "There are many mothers who will not take more than a part-time job in order to spend more time at home, but many find that they must do some work in order to help their husbands pay the high rents of the new flats or council cottages and keep up the extras to which they have become accustomed..."

In 1956 observers at St.Mildred's attributed some blame for the break-up of families to the housing shortage, referring to: "...the young wife with one or more babies cooped up within the same four walls day in, day out, the young husband returning at night to a nervous atmosphere instead of the relaxation of a home. The many appeals we received.."can you find us somewhere to live, we have got to move", or "my wife is threatening to leave home, she can't stand it any longer" and we are unable to help a great deal."

The St.Mildred's workers saw the down-side of Island life. For others, family and neighbourhood life continued much as before. Diana Luckman, Island midwife in 1959, found: "...many of the families were large, very large – some had eight or more children and I actually delivered someone's eighteenth. The majority of babies were born at home and most of the children, even at the age of 10 or 11, knew that these babies arrived in the nurse's blue bag....The Island had a very good news network. Family ties were strong and grandmothers were all important...In terms of money, the people didn't have much. Certainly, on the Island, most of the homes were clean

Top picture opposite: Golden Wedding party for Alf and Lizzie Rangecroft, includes Sophie Anderson, front right, 1972. Lower picture opposite: Family party for Mrs Flo Edmunds, centre back, in St.John's Church Hall, 1964. Flo lived in Oak House, Manchester Road.

and warm and everyone was welcoming. A pillow in a drawer was a cheap substitute for a cot. Most clothes were made – I don't think there was much in the way of baby clothes' shops. In spite of families being so large, the children belonged and there was a tremendous sense of community…".

Betty Nesbitt grew up in Preston's Road in the 1950s and 1960s: "My Gran lived round the corner in Gaselee Street, an ideal close family living just yards away from one another – sheer bliss."

There were extended families who stayed in the area: "I was married in St.Luke's church in 1962. My husband lived in Glengarnock Avenue with his Grandparents until we married, this was Maud and Ben Hurr, they had lived on the Island all their lives, they remained in Glengarnock until they passed away in the 1960s. My own parents remained in Cuba Street until 1970, then they had to move to No.2 Castalia Street in Cubitt Town. My mum stayed there until she died aged 81, my father stayed for four more years then came to live with me in Hornchurch." (Island woman)

The final break-up of the old neighbourhoods took time: "Between Cuba Street and Janet Street I had 37 close relatives. They had all been born on the Island. Most left when the houses were pulled down in 1964." Mrs P. Barrs (nee Mackay). At this time (mid-1960s) there was still work available locally – it was the re-housing that broke up neighbourhoods, before unemployment took hold, as Peter Wright's story shows. Born in Tooke Street and a pupil at the old St.Luke's School in Westferry Road, he started work in 1965 as a draughtsman with Bedford and Son Ltd., at the top of the street. So did some of his school mates from surrounding streets, but, as he said: "…by the time we all worked there, we had been re-housed out of the area."

With the decline of the extended family and neighbourhood networks, the care for the sick, the elderly and the lonely which had been given between relatives and neighbours also dwindled, although it did not disappear completely. Contact had been lost and, between strangers, was difficult to renew. Cars, televisions and comfortable homes made life more private and at the same time, there were new problems on the council estates: single parents, separated couples, lonely old people.

In the 1970s a change in Government policy brought the era of council house building to an end. Local authority budgets were cut and repair and maintenance on existing stock began to suffer. Some Island council homes became hard to let. Poverty was widespread again, as it had been in the 1920s; in 1976, the income of Islanders averaged 13% less per household than the average for the rest of London. People were not keen to move to the Island with its poor transport, uncertain schooling and rising unemployment.

But the housing crisis in London was deepening and so for some, there was no option but a high-rise flat on the Isle of Dogs In 1972 Herbert Murray wrote an article "Going to the Dogs" or the *Guide Bleu to London's Isle of Dogs*, in which he described the newcomers who, decanted, or "lured" into new estates on the Barkantine and Samuda: "…are used to mainland facilities, mainland prices, mainland schools and bus services and they have not lived all their lives with that infernal swing bridge."

The purchase of council homes by their tenants had been a growing trend since the 1960s and was now further encouraged. Some Islanders were able to buy their own homes for the first time, the downside of this being that the overall stock of council housing was thereby reduced, as no additions were being made. At the same time, the first private housing aimed at the professional middle class market, appeared in Capstan Square and Saunders Ness Road. A new kind of resident, such as teachers, architects, journalists and lawyers, came to live on the Island and, in some cases, to contribute to local life. They were the vanguard.

10. Social and community Life Post-War to the 1970s

In the changing world of the 1950s and 1960s the Island's continuing isolation from the rest of the East End meant that local facilities were still in great demand – a demand which was not always met by existing provision. Rising living standards and shorter working hours now gave people a degree of leisure and freedom from want which they had never known before. Many, both established Islanders and newcomers, turned their attention to protecting and improving local amenities, so that, as council housing estates rose from the rubble left behind by the Blitz, new forms of self-help and local action seemed to rise within the new community as it took shape.

The Island's traditional neighbourliness survived where it could, especially where people still lived at street level. Joan C., writing about her childhood, said:

"I was born in 1946 and have always lived on the Isle of Dogs. When I was a child I lived in Alpha Grove and can remember the warmth and love shown to and by everyone I knew. Doors were always open and even though money was scarce nobody would ever think of stealing from their neighbour (maybe the docks, yes, but not a neighbour). I remember the smell of polish in the old St.Luke's School and the gleaming brass door handles. I remember the call of the

Opposite: George Pye senior, stevedore. George had an allotment on the Mudchute and at the Allotments Society show in the mid 1960s, he fulfilled a cherished ambition, winning all six classes with his potatoes.

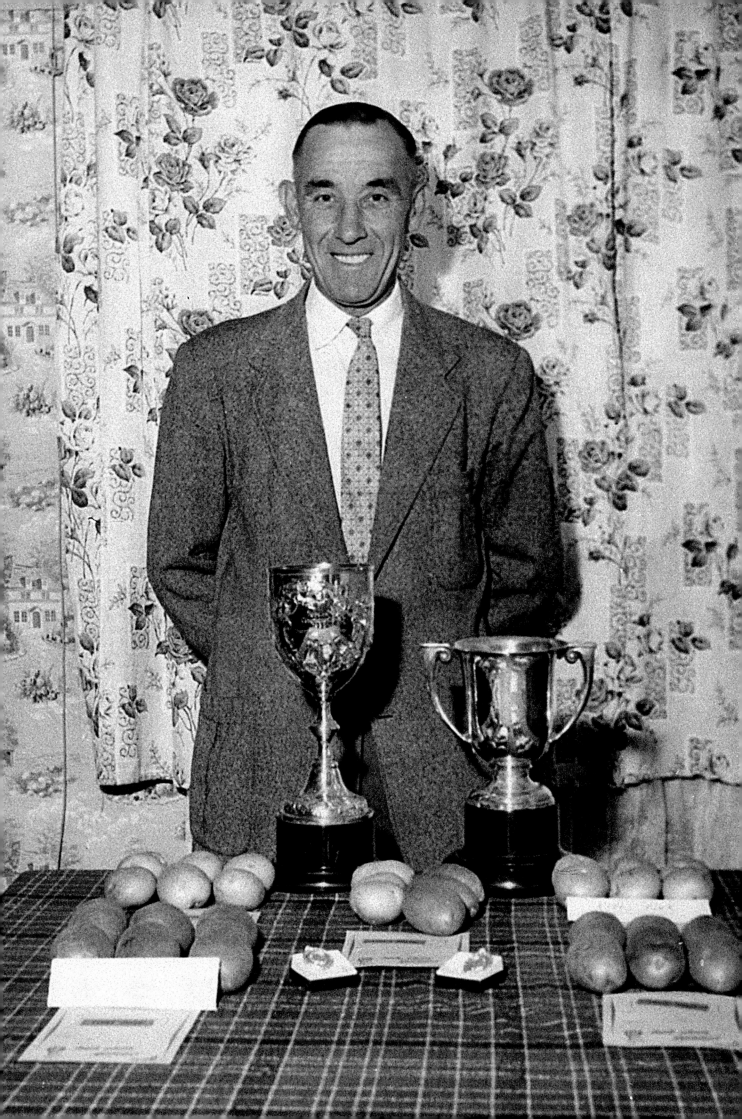

coalman and rag and bone man – and the winkleman on Sundays. I can still see the whitened steps and the gleaming clean windows. I remember all the neighbours and friends helping each other out in times of need and never made a song and dance about it because they didn't have to impress anyone, we were all on the same boat."

Amanda Rainger, who came to live in Harbinger Road in 1971, found a sense of community in the terraced street: "...cuppas when I had no electricity, cuttings for my garden, offers to feed the cat, let the telly man in, push my car...I too had my part to play. When our milkman died, I was asked to compose the official street letter to the widow." She noted the "caring net which still spread over the Island in the best East End tradition." In the warm summer of 1976: "older residents sat on kitchen chairs on the pavement outside their open front door, chatting to each other....In 1977 we had a great Jubilee Party, organised by two wonderful mums who started a door-to-door collection months before".

The re-housing of Islanders, and the re-housing of people from other parts of London onto the Island in the post-war decades, meant that there was very varied experience of community life. Those with local connections found it easier to settle than the newcomers, who, especially if they found themselves on the 10th floor of a block of flats with poor public transport to other parts of London, could experience the Island as isolated and the people as unfriendly. Support was available from the welfare state. By 1977 the new social services in George Green Centre provided help for "the less able members of the community like children, elderly, physically and mentally handicapped and the mentally ill...support included daily childminders and pre-school playgroups, home helps and meals on wheels or luncheon clubs; services for the blind, partially sighted, the deaf and physically handicapped." But these services were often overstretched and many people, especially older residents, felt a sense of abandonment:

"We were happy, happier than we are today, I tell you, 'cos you had friends then. You haven't got 'em now. You could have your door shut and they wouldn't care if you was dead or alive. In them days, your door was always open. You didn't feel that you wasn't wanted, sort of thing."

Schools, churches, sports and community groups and pubs all played a part in easing the way for newcomers and in forging new bonds of friendship, especially amongst young people who met initially at school and went on to become members of local youth clubs.

The war, the 1944 Education Act and post-war re-building, brought many changes to Island schools. Only St.Edmund's and Harbinger remained largely unaffected. St.John's Church of England School was destroyed by the Blitz. Cubitt Town School, built in Saunders Ness Road in 1935, was blown up by a land-mine. Millwall Central and the Isle of Dogs School were damaged beyond repair. St.Luke's and Glengall Road School also suffered damage.

It was many years before Island schools were re-built and re-organised to provide a modern education system for the second half of the century. And this was only achieved through the vigorous expression of strong local discontent with the delays and shortcomings which were experienced.

Children were now required to have separate education at secondary level, and soon after the war, the old Glengall Road Elementary School became the Island's first Secondary School. Junior pupils from Glengall Road were allocated to other schools, including Cubitt Town, rebuilt in 1951.

In the immediate post-war years St.Luke's seemed much the same; the same building, the same desks with china ink-wells, the same coke fires and iron fireguards, the same celebration of Holy Days at church. St.Luke's was still part of the small community of Millwall families who had survived the war and lived in the battered streets round about. Jean Beckley (nee Bullock), recalled "Looking back now, the friends you made in the classroom were the same friends you had outside of school and everything we did, church, school and social events, were all, it seemed in some way connected to St.Luke's."

New house-building on Millwall continued into the mid-1960s. By that time it was clear that the old St.Luke's was inadequate in every way, with its tiny playground and Victorian classrooms, and its location on a busy road next to industrial sites. The London Diocesan Board sold the school to the nearby timber firm, Lenanton's, and with government grants, bought another school in a different part of the Island. This was the former Cubitt Town School, in Saunders Ness Road. Meanwhile, the education authority decided to build a new school on Millwall, the present Seven Mills.

Pupils and teachers at Cubitt Town School had to move to make way for St.Luke's. The authorities decided to close Glengall Road Secondary School and transfer the pupils to the new St.Paul's Way Comprehensive School. This made room for Cubitt

Top picture opposite: Seven Mills School in the 1970s, including Keith Medleycott, Luke Starus, Trudy Coveley, Susan Donnerland, Stacy English, Madeleine Haines, Debbie Hogger, Andrew Boylett, Tony Harrison, Dennis Colliero, Duncan Victoria and Michael Onslow.

Lower picture: Dockland Settlement tap-dancing class, 1967, run by Marie Smith and her daughter (back row). Also includes Pat Goodwin, Kim Clark, Christine Lilley, Susan Evans, Jackie Moran, Leslie Coyle, Cheryl Hughes, Michelle Hayes and Velda Hughes.

Town School to move into the old Glengall Road building – once it had been refurbished. The situation which then arose – with secondary school pupils having to travel on and off the Island, one large Island school closed for refurbishment and other junior schools full to bursting – was one of the factors which led to the "Unilateral Declaration of Independence" on the Isle of Dogs in March 1970.

This brought local issues to the fore and the school change-over took place in September 1971. Cubitt Town School moved into its present home in the old Glengall Road building, and St.Luke's took over its new home in Saunders Ness Road. It was not until 1977 that the Island's new comprehensive school was opened (see below).

Island schools were also used in the evenings for adult education and recreation. At the new Seven Mills School on Millwall, the church magazine for 1971 recorded that: "At night the school wakes up and opens it doors...to the parents, friends, old age pensioners living around the school....to learn more about needlework, carpentry, cooking or just chatting over a cup of tea..."

St.Mildred's Settlement was rehoused after the war in Hammond House then in St.Luke's vicarage where it ran activities for children in the 1950s. By the early 1960s St.Mildred's had a purpose-built house in Castalia Square, with two new workers, June Winfield and Jean Connock, and they continued to run clubs for juniors and teenagers, Sunday schools and confirmation classes, with welfare work now largely confined to visiting the sick.

St.Luke's Church had been badly damaged in the war but the Vicarage, the church hall, and the congregation all survived. Both St.Luke's and Christ Church offered rambles, guides and brownies, weekend trips to holiday cottages, football, gymnastics, cricket, sewing groups, debating groups, children's country holidays. The Mother's Club, in addition to the usual outings, debated such issues as "Television is a waste of time" and "The English race in these modern days does not work so hard". Catherine Newberry joined Christ Church Youth Club and joined in all the activities, including "a regular pantomime in season." She later married another club member.

A Youth Club party at St.Luke's in 1956 was described in a parish magazine: "...the feminine members invaded the kitchen to cook, whilst the more strenuous males denuded the common room of its

St.Paul's Church women's group Christmas party in the 1950s. Members of the Youth Club waited at table and they are, standing at the back, Eileen Mason, Frieda Newman and Shirley Knights. Also in the picture: Mrs Hathaway, Mrs Lockwood, Pat Garland, Eileen Gooding, Mrs Farman, Mrs Phillips, Mrs Dixon, Mrs Garland, Mrs Coombs and Margaret Mills.

furniture then all seated themselves on the carpet in front of a roaring fire and armed with fork and plate demolished masses of sausage and mash and drank fruit squash. Superior criticism of the cooks by the lads, games and jollification ended a successful evening."

Times were changing fast and by 1957 the Parish Youth Notes in the magazine had to admit that: "Rock 'n' Roll sessions in St.Luke's and Christ Church Halls are rapidly becoming popular. Remember – first Christ Church: Evening 6.30; St.Luke's: Mission Service, 7.30. Rock 'n' Roll in the Halls after the services."

Marion Hesselden recalled that being a teenager on the Island in the 1960s was "great":

"We had the Dockland Settlement, where the highlight of the evening was a bottle of coke, bag of crisps, Beatles' records and table tennis. St. Luke's had a thriving youth group and we produced the play *Sweeney Todd*. Some of us went to a German youth camp in the Black Forest in 1966, quite an adventure as continental travel was not common.

Those living in the southern half of Millwall had a choice of two clubs: St.Paul's, or the Dockland Settlement. Eddie Stone, who wrote that: "...the Youth Club was the centre of most young Islanders' lives", joined the former, although he admitted Dockland had: "...superior amenities, for example, they often had dances on a Saturday night."

Members of St.Paul's would attend these dances, not without some friendly rivalry about dancing with one of "theirs" as opposed to one of "ours". St.Paul's club was open four nights a week and provided "snooker, table tennis, darts, gymnastics and the latest records played on a radiogram. Saturday afternoon was the highlight of the week for the club's football team members, with a league or cup match at Hackney cheered on by the Reverend Jimmy Little. On Sundays we met in a small hall above church for talks, quizzes and mildly religious activities. Unofficially we would exchange experiences of whatever dance we had attended the previous night."

The Presbyterian Church owned a large house and grounds named "Dormers" at Broxbourne. Club members went there twice a year for a long weekend. The girls slept in the house, the boys in the barn, and youth leader Margo slept in the house to make sure there were no midnight comings and goings. She was very good at organising a rota for washing up, scrubbing vegetables, and other unpopular jobs, in such a way that it brought together members who wanted to be together, thus ensuring few complaints."

During the 1960s the Dockland Settlement in East Ferry Road continued to host youth activities including fencing, sailing, fishing, football, stamp collecting and the arts and to provide outings and holidays for all ages. Millwall Pigeon Racing club, the 6th Poplar Scout Group, and 1st City of London

Army Cadet Unit were all housed within the Settlement, which had also helped in founding the Isle of dogs Sea Cadet Unit.

Although memories and records present an optimistic picture, this is only partial. Some places of worship, clubs and societies were broken up by the war when call-up and evacuation scattered the membership. The Alpha Grove Methodist chapel, still standing after the war, became a community centre when the area around it had been completely pulled down and rebuilt.

The congregation of Cubitt Town Primitive Methodist Chapel was decimated by the Second World War but continued to meet in small numbers. When Island House Church and Community Centre was opened in Castalia Square in 1972 the remaining Cubitt Town Methodists were given a home there. A leading member, Mrs Warwick, became famous for her weekly charity stall at Island House, where for many years she sold bric-a-brac in aid of the London Hospital.

St.Paul's Presbyterian Church also had a dwindling congregation post-war, and they also moved into Island House Church and Community Centre in Castalia Square, whilst the old church was taken over for industrial storage.

Church, chapel and the pub, were all declining in popularity in the face of Sunday outings by car (including visiting scattered relatives) and more comfortable homes, where the television was rapidly replacing all traditional forms of entertainment. Sports retained their popularity. There were fewer adult football teams than formerly, since there were less companies and public houses to support them, but youth football thrived in and out of school. Parents and teenagers gave their time and energy to supporting and promoting young teams. Millwall Youth Football Club was formed in 1952 by Tony Parsons who at the age of 14 gathered some lads and ran what was basically a street team, playing against other Island sides on the red ochre pitch in Millwall Park. The club entered the East London Youth Clubs Football League and grew to have, at one stage, 12 sides, from under-elevens to seniors. Their high standards of play won them many League Championships and Cup Winners' medals and a number of players from the club became professionals. They had a role model in Ivor Broadis, who grew up on the Island, played for Tottenham and Millwall, served as a wartime bomber pilot and later played for Manchester City and Newcastle United.

The lure of stardom was also a glittering prize in boxing, and here again, it all sprang from self-help and local initiative. George Attewell was a member of the Island Amateur Sporting Club in the 1960s:

"It was made up of local people, there was me, Jimmy Batten, old Jimmy Batten that is, young Jimmy had not even turned pro then, Dinny Hill, Micky

Duhig, Terry Duhig, my brother Patsy, Kenny Bender, Dickie Richardson... we done a lot of charity work, I was one of the people who could go round this Island and collect money off businesses and pubs..."

The club provided the training ground for young boxers like Tony and Jimmy Batten (born 1954 and 1955 in Mellish Street, later moving to Parsonage Street). In their early teens these lads joined the Poplar and District Boxing Club in Vernon Hall, Roman Road, where they boxed in club shows and occasionally represented the London schools in national and international championships. Tony retired at 15, but Jimmy, now a member of the West Ham Boys' Club in Plaistow, went on to win six national titles at junior level. He turned professional at 18 and at 21 won the light middle-weight championship of Great Britain. After winning two more title fights he became the owner of a Lonsdale belt, one of boxing's highest accolades. After further success in The United States and Britain, Jimmy retired at 28.

Rowing was another sport which was locally organised and in the 1960s the Poplar, Blackwall and District Rowing Club launched a successful appeal for funds to pay for a new boathouse on the corner of Ferry Street and Saunders Ness Road near Island Gardens.

The North Greenwich Bowls Club had to move from Island Gardens, where the green had been damaged beyond repair during the Blitz. A new green and pavillion were provided by the London County Council in 1956.

Those pubs which were left standing after the Blitz were lively and popular, if a bit run down. The war had brought greater social freedom and women were seen in pubs more frequently, though not on their own. They had started smoking too – women of that generation remember starting to smoke at work, or during the war.

Many pubs still housed local clubs – Millwall Albion football club's headquarters was the *Pride of the Isle* for a time, then they moved to the *Magnet and Dewdrop* and later the *Robbie Burns*. In the 1950s and 1960s live music was provided by local groups. Lorry driver Jack Rump remembered the days of skiffle, the national craze of the late 1950s, a gift to the amateur with its three-chord guitars and a bass constructed from a tea-chest, a broom handle and a piece of string:

"I always did like singing, I started off singing at Crystal Palace, a thousand voices, when I was at school, but it was my son, he was doing it when he was a kid about eleven years old, where he was evacuated. And anyhow he used to do it when he was a lorry driver, doing his loads up to Manchester and that and he used to take his guitar with him and sit

Cubitt Town School, three members of the football team, 1968-69: Terry Martin, Barry Gittos and Micky Burkey.

On the foreshore in Ferry Street, old North Greenwich Railway Station in the background: christening a new boat for the Poplar, Blackwall and District Rowing Club, includes Mr and Mrs Woodard Fisher and Bill Smith.

1950s skiffle group, on left, Jack Rump junior and on the right, his father Jack.

on the back of the lorry and do all the skiffle songs and all that. Well, I was similar to him, but I done all these pubs round here and others over at Rotherhithe and Bermondsey, we used to do all them. The group was going a long while and we called that "Pop's Group", that was me. I used to go with Jack (his friend). I painted an old tea chest up, like a dice. That tea chest went everywhere, Devon and all over the place, all over the country. I was on a big timber lorry and I made a stage out of some old timber. I used to meet Jack when I'd finished me loads of a Friday night. Jack and me and the son-in-law, had about three car loads and we used to have a bit of entertainment in the pubs, take the guitar and anyone who could play piano....The skiffle, the box, that was pretty simple that was. It was just bomp bomp bomp, like. And everyone was doing that."

Betty Nesbitt remembered her youth in the 1960s as being: "...quite eventful; lots of Beatles' music, parties, and pub crawls round the Island in my new high heels – we used to dress up in those days". It was in these "swinging 'sixties" that the *Newcastle Arms*, renamed the *Waterman's Arms* by landlord Dan Farsons, became a celebrity venue and a fashionable night spot for trendy young Londoners.

In the 1970s Island pubs offered the following entertainment: old-time music and dancing at the *Lord Nelson* every Friday and Saturday; Go-go Girls every night at *The Vulcan*, live music at the *Tooke Arms* on Friday and Saturday; and "Drag Every Night" at the *City Arms* – this was also the chief attraction at *The Londoner* in West India Dock Road. The traditional combination of a piano and group singing carried on in Island pubs until the 1980s.

Workplace friendships remained important, as already shown (Chapter 8). Ursula Marchant emphasised: "Most of all I remember the many

The last night in the pub Princess of Wales (known as Mac's) in Manchester Road, Mrs Muggleton, Ronny Emms and Daisy Franklin. Pub demolished to make room for the George Green Centre.

friends I made whilst working at Fenner and Alders" the paint company where she started in 1947. Island firms still provided outings and entertainment. Betty Nesbitt's father worked at Badcocks, where she recalled the Christmas parties which the firm used to arrange in the hall of Glengall Road School. However, the scattering of the workforce through re-housing meant there was less opportunity for socialising outside working hours.

For all the self-help and initiative which Islanders and new residents showed in rebuilding community life after the war and into the prosperous decade of the 1960s, there was a limit to what they could achieve. Transport, housing and schooling remained neglected areas of everyday life and these were issues which needed the intervention and support of the local authorities. For people who wanted better amenities, one possibility was to move away. But many

people did not have, or did not want, this option, either because they chose to stay conveniently close to work and relatives, or because, once newly-settled on the Island, they needed some stability for themselves and their families. But they were increasingly aware that standards of local services were falling behind the rest of London.

The 1950s was a period of recovery and slow rebuilding. In the 1960s, as wages and living standards improved everywhere, a sense of neglect and injustice began to be felt on the Island. Many people were still living in run-down housing or were paying high rents for new homes. There was no sign of better public transport; schooling provision seemed to be worsening, with a shortage of secondary school places for the Island's expanding population. And the local authorities were perceived as slow to act, whilst by comparison, other areas of the East End, and other parts of London, were seen to be getting a bigger share of resources. This sense of grievance was heightened in 1965 when with a restructuring of local government, Poplar Borough Council was absorbed into the London Borough of Tower Hamlets and the number of Island councillors was reduced from six to two.

Speaking about the 1950s and 1960s, one of the Island's foremost campaigners for local democracy, Ted Johns, interviewed in 1980, remarked that there had been a change in the nature of the local council, and in attitudes towards it, brought about by a decline in radical politics and the merging of small local councils into a larger unit. "At that time, in the 1960s when they formed Tower Hamlets, the identity of Poplar, as being the radical Poplar, if you like, began actually to disappear. Among the representatives, they were no longer the men of the streets, they became men of the Town Hall, they became administrators."

And it was during this period that action groups emerged on the Island to challenge the authorities from outside the established forum of local politics. These groups drew in people of all ages and backgrounds – both established families and newcomers – and were built on the existing traditions of neighbourliness, trade unionism, self help and a strong sense of place. The groups took a variety of forms and were primarily pressure groups concerned with improving local conditions; they adopted a range of methods in their campaigns and in many instances were extremely successful.

Top picture opposite: When politics was fun too... A Christmas get-together for Poplar Labour Party in the 1960s, includes Nellie Cressall.

Lower picture: Millwall Residents' Association New Year Dance, attended by 500 people; left to right: George and Flo Donns, Ernie and Ivy Harris, Ivy Willson (in white), Sid Freeman, George James, Louise Bowater; at the back, Alf Matthews, Bill Willson.

View of Millwall Dock Inner Basin in the 1960s, with the celebrated "Glass Bridge" linking Glengall Grove and Tiller Road. Brunswick Wharf Power Station in the background.

Millwall Residents' Association was born in the late 1950s, partly around a campaign to retain the footbridge over the Millwall Dock, which the Port of London Authority proposed to close. Their plan was very unpopular with Islanders who flocked to join the MRA, under the leadership of John Pratt, Bill Willson and the Reverend and Mrs Freeman of St.Luke's Church. Membership mounted into hundreds, two thousand people signed the petition for the reinstatement of a road bridge as well as retention of the footbridge, and the forces of the unions, the Borough Council, the London County Council and the local MP were brought into play against the PLA.

Faced with this kind of opposition the PLA conceded defeat, but only over the pedestrian right-of-way. This was retained as a high level walkway, the "Glass Bridge".

The six local Borough Councillors now withdrew their backing for the roadbridge and switched their support to the PLA, an important local employer and ratepayer. Feelings continued to run high. Islanders opposed the plans for the elevated walkway with its lifts and long corridor over the docks, rightly foreseeing that it would become a target for vandalism. They were outraged at local Councillors' change of sides. Membership of the MRA continued to grow and before long a separate group was formed, Cubitt Town Residents' Association, later the Island Tenants' Association. The ITA had a "Local Youth" branch and Janet Hill (nee Price) was one of the founder members in 1965. She recalled that for one shilling and sixpence membership fee, "...the club provided a meeting place where we could play table tennis, listen to records and buy soft drinks. we also ran events such as dances and charity walks, and a memorable day-trip to Clacton, for which we had to hire a double-decker bus, there were so many keen to go".

The "battle for the bridge" may have been lost but an important victory had been gained in the discovery of the potential political power of local association. In 1962, three ITA representatives – L.Towler, R.Gaylor and J.Coleman – took all three seats for Cubitt Town in the Borough Council elections, the first time in 34 years that the Poplar Borough Council had not been solidly Labour. In 1964 the ITA took both seats on the newly-formed Tower Hamlets Council. Meanwhile the most active members of the Millwall Residents Association had managed to make their peace with the Council.

Millwall Residents' Association met on the first Wednesday of every month at St.Paul's Hall, Westferry Road. In 1965 their officers were: Secretary W.F.Willson, Chairman J.W.Vicat and Treasurer Cllr.E.T.Johns. Members of the committee included: "A works manager, stevedores, a tally clerk, checker, retired insurance executive, lorry driver, housewife, toolmaker, electrician, ships' clerk and lighterman".

In the early 1960s, the LCC plan for all secondary school children to travel off the Island aroused the anger of parents. This was at a time when the Island's other primary schools were still old and run-down.

Under the chairmanship of the articulate and well-informed John Franklin, of Thermopylae Gate, a committee was formed to challenge the plan. Committee members conducted a survey of 908 homes and demonstrated convincingly that within a few years the number of secondary school children on the Island would more than justify the expense of a new school. The campaigners also carried out a traffic census, which allowed them to argue that the narrow exit roads were congested and quite unsafe for children to use as cycle routes. The limited bus services were already crowded at peak times, and: "It would take 18 completely empty buses to transport the secondary pupils alone". The detailed records of their findings reveal the amount of dedicated work undertaken by local volunteers in collecting this information.

The campaigners' efforts led them from their local councillors, to their MP, Ian Mikardo, to the highest levels of the Inner London Education Authority and finally to the Minister of Education. John Franklin recalled that it was only when the Conservative opposition in ILEA was drawn into the conflict that the authorities finally accepted that the Island should have its own secondary school. On June 28th, 1977, the ceremonial opening of the George Green Centre took place. Built alongside Island Gardens across the remains of Barque Street, Brig Street and Ship Street, the Centre incorporated George Green Comprehensive School, the Lansbury Adult Education Institute, Social Services, Community Services, a Youth Centre, a Day Centre for the elderly, a Day Nursery and a Sports and Leisure Centre.

Building on the success of the schools' campaign, and the experiences gained, many individuals involved in this and other early campaigns remained active in the community for many years, taking a leading role

1965, Polling Day at a by-election for a vacant seat on Tower Hamlets Council, with councillors Dick Gaylor and Len Jordan.

in local organisations and in some cases becoming independent councillors. The Island representatives on the Council were successful in keeping otherwise neglected issues, such as provision for education and transport, in the public eye, always with the active support of numerous individuals. The 1970s, the decade of closures and rising unemployment, witnessed some successful campaigns around local issues as well as the formation of other local groups, particularly the tenants' associations on the newer housing estates such as St.John's and Samuda. This brought into community life people who had moved to the Island from elsewhere in London, with their different experiences and higher expectations.

The Isle of Dogs achieved a brief notoriety when on 1st March, 1970, a group of people barricaded the bridges, effectively closing road access between the Island and the rest of London for several hours. In their "Unilateral Declaration of Independence", it was stated that Islanders would pay no more taxes until better schools, transport and other facilities were provided. TV cameras and journalists from the big daily papers descended on the Island, and the Island's problems were effectively brought to national attention, too much so for some who were highly critical of the demonstration.

In 1972 Herbert Murray wrote of the Island as enjoying "a celebrated obscurity", where for the resident: "...life was hard. And for the council, it is a headache." He described the poor state of transport, shops and schools "inadequate because it is held that the community is not large enough to support them". The residents he talked to complained of high grocery prices, isolation, and having to walk three miles home from a late night because they have missed the last bus.

The Association of Island Communities (AIC) was formed in 1969, and under its umbrella the TAs joined forces with all other local organisations, schools and churches. Member groups included: Alpha Pensioners' Association, Lansbury Institute, London City Mission, North Greenwich Bowling Club, Poplar District Scouting Association, St.Paul's church, Samuda Residents' Association, the Dockland Settlement, Island Churches' Youth Clubs and the Parochial Church Council. The AIC had a full-time officer in Ted Johns, and an office at 151 Manchester Road, which also housed an advice centre.

The AIC's objectives were to "promote recreation and leisure time occupations...for the people of the Isle of Dogs" and "to bring together people and organisations in a common effort to advance education and to provide facilities in the interests of social welfare". This statement is a measure of how little faith the community had in the local authority's willingness to provide such facilities, and signalled a strong commitment to self-help and independence. The AIC's first Annual Report highlighted the need for better communications, such as a regular Newsletter, within the Island community,

Community campaigners from the Isle of Dogs in the 1970s, on a demonstration at the Town Hall, with goats from the Mudchute Park and Farm.

Picture opposite:
Foundation stone, designed by Ted Johns, for the new Island House Church and Community Centre, opened in Roserton Street in January 1972.

and for "people on the Island to keep a very close watching brief on what the planners are and are not doing."

The Islander newspaper was first published in the mid-1970s. It reflected the activities of the Isle of Dogs Action Group, other local groups and the work of the AIC, in local campaigns against the Southern Relief Road and housing on the Mudchute, and for better transport, education and housing. The paper also gave voice to individual views on local issues and debated the future of employment at a time when the

docks were threatened with closure and industries were moving out.

For all the community action and achievements of the 1970s, there was one key area in which nothing could be done to stop the coming changes. The London and St.Katherine Docks had closed in 1965. During the 1970s, in a climate of protests, strikes, meetings and appeals, the prospect of further dock closure came ever nearer, together with the "knock-on" effect of unemployment in other workplaces. The numerous plans for the area which were drawn up during the 1970s each added another layer to the veils of uncertainty which clouded the future of people living on the Island and in Docklands generally. Writing in *The Times* in 1977, Norman Shrapnel described the Island as: "...full of questions...about its past, its present, its future...".

When the London Docklands Development Corporation was created by the Conservative Government in 1980, it was opposed in the House of Lords by petitioners from the areas affected. The arguments of the opposition focussed on the undemocratic nature of the new agency and its lack of local accountability. But the House of Lords ruled, in effect, that up to then, experience had shown that local interests were part of the problem, and so the opposition was defeated.

The northern end of Preston's Road in the early 1980s. The "Welcome" mural dates from the 1970s, the graffiti is a comment on the new development. A photograph by Mike Seaborne.

11. Twenty Years of Change.

The Island seemed green and peaceful in 1980. The roads were quiet. It was easy to cycle or walk past the housing estates with their rows of parked cars and small shops, past the corrugated iron fences which concealed abandoned wharves and factories. The Blue Bridge was rarely raised and the 56 bus ran round the Island unhindered by "bridgers" or traffic jams. Above the roofs of the warehouses on the North Quay of the West India Docks, dozens of cranes fringed the skyline, all absolutely still. The broken windows of the Glass Bridge across Millwall Dock provided a view over the silent lorry parks and the dock waters, empty except for a few abandoned barges afloat amidst scatterings of polystyrene rubbish.

And all this was about to change in ways which seemed to threaten the lifestyles of existing residents without offering them any promise of a share in a better future.

"The Canary Island...I think it's awful. Our road – have you noticed our roads? Well, there was a survey coming round, perhaps a couple of months ago. Two fellows knocked on my door, and I don't always answer the door, you know. So I looked through the curtains to see who they were. Oh, I thought, they look official. And they said, Madam, we're on a survey of the Canary Wharf. Can we approach you on the subject? So he said, What do you think of it? So I said, Not much. He said, I beg your pardon? I said, Have you seen our roads? I said. They're appalling with all these heavy vehicles that come in. And I said, all the buildings that are going up, I said, How many of the local people have you employed? Very few. So he said, Well, I wouldn't know. Well, I do, I said, I live on the Island. If you've employed a dozen, that's a lot. And I said, Who wants those big monstrosities, the Americans are going to put up? I said. None of us want that. Well, I mean, its going to be an eye-sore but they're still going on with it. 'Course, we thought it fell through, but they're still going on with it. No, I'm not agreeable with all this. And they're building houses, not for the working-class. The price they're charging, ninety-six thousand. Build houses for the local people!" (Mrs Warwick, April 1987)

For anyone living on the Isle of Dogs, the last twenty years of the twentieth century were dominated by the effects of redevelopment. There was no escaping the high level of impact from the construction of new transport systems, acres of modern apartments and skyscraper office blocks. As the last manufacturing jobs were disappearing, hundreds of workers migrated to the Island to work

Waste and desolation in the docks, early 1980s.

in banking, publishing and financial services and the resident population grew to include ethnic and occupational diversity. Local amenities improved slowly and divisions between rich and poor were underlined by conflicts over employment and housing.

Responses to these changes from people living on the Island varied, from outrage, vandalism and reasoned opposition, to co-operation, acceptance and indifference. Councillors and community leaders on the Island and in Docklands generally, were frustrated and angry at the absence of consultation, the lack of consideration for local needs and the arbitrary nature of the development process. Overall, there was sufficient positive response to make a real

September 1985, undeveloped land opposite Canary Wharf, West India Docks.

difference to the process of change, but observers remained critical of the one-sided nature of the development, especially in its early stages when the focus was entirely on attracting private investment without consideration for the social needs of the resident population.

The London Docklands Development Corporation arrived quietly, setting up a base in the former offices of the Olsen Line, one of the last shipping companies to invest in the Millwall Docks. The "red brick road" was laid through the dock area, which was opened to the public for the first time. The roadsides were planted with dozens of London plane trees, and the habitat of the fishes and birds which lived in the dock basins was protected. Old warehouses and sheds were pulled down, cranes and

The arrival of ASDA transformed local shopping.

other quayside equipment were dismantled. The first low-rise office buildings, in bright colours and modern designs, appeared around the Inner Basin of the Millwall Dock. A bigger sewerage system was installed and a striking new Pumping Station was built in Stewart Street. Limehouse Studios opened in the old warehouses on Canary Wharf, bringing television productions into the heart of the Island. An estate of small houses was built on Friars Mead, adjacent to the Mudchute and close to ASDA Superstore, which was opened in 1983.

Abandoned riverside factories were taken over for redevelopment. Lorries laden with rubble trundled back and forth, clogging the roads and leaving trails of mud behind them. Luxury houses and apartment blocks, with restaurants and private health clubs, rose up to replace the old industries. The Dockland Clipper bus route was opened and in 1987 the innovative Docklands Light Railway started running, putting Islanders within a few minutes travel of the heart of London. When the Corporation moved out of the former Olsen's shed, it was rebuilt to house the London Arena as a new sports and entertainment venue for the capital.

There were setbacks, but the redevelopment of the Isle of Dogs was an unstoppable gravy train. In the late 1980s the Canary Wharf proposal came on the scene. It seemed an impossible project, but within months, Limehouse Studios had been demolished and tall towers were rising from the mud of the former dock basins, their pinnacles reaching the clouds which are reflected in their shining sides. The transformation of the environment continued into the 1990s with the construction of West Ferry Circus and the Limehouse Link road. The latter was tunneled underground to preserve what remained of the "historic riverside hamlet" and many people had to be re-housed. These gigantic projects raised the amount of noise, dust and general disruption to unbearable levels, especially for people in Limehouse and Poplar to the north of the Island. "The character has gone from Poplar and in its place is dirt and violence..." said Maud Marks, summing up how people felt.

Two people died, many were injured and everyone on the Island was shaken by the explosion of an IRA bomb at South Quay Station on 9th February, 1996. The light railway was temporarily put out of action, and residents in the Barkantine Estate had to wait months before their homes were repaired. One result was tighter security on and around Canary Wharf, police checkpoints on all the approach roads.

The notorious "bridgers" returned as building materials were transported into the dock area and tons of rubble were shifted out in the humble barge, brought back from retirement. Meanwhile, work continued on the Docklands Light Railway, with longer trains and platforms, then an extension to Beckton and another to Lewisham. This latter project brought disruption to the southern end of the Island as East Ferry Road and Millwall Park became

Cows on the Mudchute before the new stable block was built.

Children at Cubitt Town School in 1985.

building sites for two new stations and a tunnel under the Thames. Also in the 1990s, the Jubilee Line Extension was built and opened, a first tube station for the Isle of Dogs providing rapid links to the centre of London and eastwards to Stratford. By the end of the century, the high-rise office blocks of Millenium Quarter were taking shape on Heron Quays, adjacent to Canary Wharf.

There were also changes to the area between the Enterprise Zone in the dock area, and the fringe of new housing development along the river's edge. In the early 1980s, when ASDA was built, the Mudchute, which by now combined allotments, wildlife areas, park, stables and farm, was landscaped with new entrances and planting. At the same time, the old Hawkins and Tipson ropewalk was turned into a long formal garden linking East Ferry Road and Stebondale Street. Later, thousands of trees and shrubs were planted in a greening and screening operation which helped to soften the impact of the high-rise buildings to the north of the Mudchute. New stables and an education centre were added.

Along Westferry Road a new Health Centre was built on the Barkantine Estate; the Island Art Centre in Tiller Road (later relocated); the Dockland Sailing Centre on the site of the Millwall Dock Bridge, was opened in 1989, and in the same year the Cedar Centre opened for multi-cultural education and recreation on Timber Wharves; St.Paul's Art Centre (The Space) was created as a performing arts venue

out of the old Scotch church. Further along the bright brickwork of the new St.Edmund's Roman Catholic church, appeared in 2000. A new health centre was built near ASDA in 1994 and another medical centre followed in Spindrift Avenue. Christ Church still stood amidst trees at the bend in Manchester Road, not far from the brand-new Police Station. The new public buildings blended in with the modern apartment blocks, intractably tidy and neat with their formal planting and fortress-like gates. To keep up appearances, the council estates were not allowed to run to seed, but were repainted and refurbished. Pubs were smartened up too, or transformed into apartments and restaurants.

The Island's schools were upgraded, as the curriculum was modernised and the population expanded. The George Green Comprehensive School grew to fill almost the entire site apart from the Day Nursery; new classrooms were added to other Island schools, St.Luke's built its own Nature Park and Learner Swimming Pool and a new Primary School was opened at Arnhem Wharf in 1994.

But older Islanders felt that there was "no sense of adventure for kids" at the beginning of the 21st century. And children sensed the constraints of living in such a densely built-up environment:

"Life's hard when you live on the Isle of Dogs especially when you're a kid because everythings made for adults, like all adults do is drive cars and all they build is roads. If you want some fun you have to get in trouble and everywhere there is signs saying NO BALL GAMES. The only place to play football is Millwall Park and there is dogs poo everywhere. I know this is the Isle of Dogs but Millwall Park is ridiculous! They build buildings that we don't need like Canary Wharf. Ben." (From *Stories from the Island*, published in 1994 by the Island Churches.)

In 1981, very little sign of the coming changes was apparent to the average Islander. Everything was words: plans, proposals, reports and meetings. Most people continued to be affected by poverty, poor transport, isolation and unemployment in the course of their daily lives. Production at the Island's remaining industrial firms was staggering to a halt. There was a bevy of closures in the early 1980s, raising the jobless total and at the same time, freeing land for redevelopment.

In 1982 McDougall's Mill, by then part of the Rank Hovis McDougall conglomerate, with the workforce down to 65, ended 120 years of production beside Millwall Dock. John Bellamy's Engineering Company had been making boilers and pressurised tanks at Byng Street for 122 years, but rates had risen

Making the last colour at Burrell's, 1984.

from £650 a year in 1951 to nearly £44,000 by 1980, the firm could not survive, and their workforce of 36 became redundant. The last days of C.& E. Morton, now just a depot for Beecham's, were approaching, as the workforce was cut from 34 to 3. And Associated Lead announced its forthcoming closure with the loss of 100 jobs on the Island; the company had decided to concentrate production in one large plant instead of several small ones.

Timber handlers Montague L. Meyer, the last big employer within the Millwall Dock area, had merged with International Timber in 1982 to form Meyer International plc. It was becoming increasingly difficult for the PLA to justify keeping Millwall Dock open for the timber ships, and so in 1983, Meyer International moved to Barking and the land was subsequently sold to a property developer.

Burrell's Millwall operation was closed in 1984, ending one hundred and fifty years of industrial

production on the site.

The redevelopment promised to bring thousands of new jobs to the Enterprise Zone – and it did. The majority required skills which redundant Islanders did not possess; or the jobs were filled by companies bringing their own workforce with them. The Docklands Light Railway had a local employment policy (there were 2,200 applicants for the first 54 jobs), and critical argument won some concessions from developers over local labour quotas, but unemployment amongst existing residents continued to rise in the 1980s. As it did so, gangs of labourers and engineers, ant-like amidst the colossal structures they were creating, obliterated the old quays and wharves beneath tons of concrete and steel. As soon as the new buildings were completed, commuters and new residents filled the high-tech offices of the financial services and publishing companies which had moved to the Isle of Dogs. Working life in this context had a completely different quality from the days when ships were repaired and cargoes were loaded and unloaded:

"I normally start about half past eight and I don't have a lunch break and I work until I finish. What I do is marketing communications...all our clients are property, construction companies, public sector, local and central government, utilities companies, all that sort of thing, and we are business advisers, so we give accounting and audit advice service, tax, merger and consulting corporate finance. So what I do is to market all of these, sell them all, promote them all, through things like publications, through PR, advertising, events, seminars, that kind of thing. So my day is incredibly varied. I have normally got about two events and three publications on the go at one time and there is ad hoc advertising and PR things that we are trying to do. So – a lot of running around, a lot of talking to people on the phone. I spend my life tied to my e-mail, tied to my laptop, and I get to go out quite a lot which is fun, obviously, because if you have got an event you are at the venue, or dealing with printers and design companies, so I do run around quite a lot." (RH, in an interview for The Ragged School Museum 1999.

Local groups, such as Docklands Forum and the Association of Island Communities, had campaigned hard since the 1970s around the need to tackle local unemployment, both by attracting companies which could use existing skills, and by retraining the redundant workforce.. Initially the Development Corporation had argued the merits of the so-called "trickle down effect" – that private investment in the area would in time, automatically create jobs for the resident population. The 1980s brought no sign of improvement. In 1987, various pressures forced the Development Corporation to change tack and it

Site clearance on Mast House Terrace, Westferry Road, 1985.

began to address the social needs of the area more directly. Millions of pounds were spent on education and training, aimed particularly at young people. It was too late for many older workers. In 1993, 27% of men were unemployed on the Isle of Dogs.

By the late 1990s there were signs that school leavers were getting jobs in the new businesses on the Island and that others were benefiting from expanding opportunities in the shops and services. But because the Island, and the London Borough of Tower Hamlets, remained a relatively deprived area, unemployment also remained high. When the Corporation handed back its area of remit to Tower Hamlets in 1997, the Borough still had "one of the highest rates of unemployment amongst working men in the country." (Palmer)

Housing was another area in which the contrast between existing residents and newcomers was keenly felt. The 1980s witnessed property boom and bust as almost anyone who could afford it climbed on the band-wagon of rising house prices to buy one of the luxury homes appearing on the Island and all over Docklands. As prices rocketed, pressure increased on the shrinking stock of public housing. People who wanted to settle close to their families felt angered by the new housing – on their doorstep but too dear to buy.

Council housing had become run down because of the use of poor quality or suspect materials (such as asbestos) and lack of resources for proper maintenance. Mould on the walls and rotting woodwork were prob-

lems which tenants could not deal with themselves. In 1987 the Isle of Dogs Neighbourhood had an allocation of one million pounds for repairs and maintenance. There were 650 units in Cubitt Town alone which required dry-lining and asbestos removal at a cost of £5,000 each, so it would be a long time before it was completed. Meanwhile Mr R., aged 75, was living in a 1920s house, confined to the ground floor, using the outside toilet, waiting to be re-housed. A young couple with a three-month old son, living in a three-bedroomed house with six other adults and two other children, had been waiting for two years to be re-housed.

Run-down flats in high-rise blocks were unpopular with tenants, but some people had little choice. The Island became home to lonely and abandoned people. Frank Horwill lived on the sixth floor of Kelson House on the Samuda Estate for a time in the 1980s, and found that the flats were used as a "dumping ground" for people who were unable to look after themselves and were neglected by the authorities either through carelessness or lack of resources. One man, who had been released from a mental institution, had been living off what he could find by picking through rubbish bins. His Social Security cheque was being sent to his brother in Hackney and he lived in the cold and darkness, with a leaking toilet, until his neighbour intervened.

Nearly everyone on the waiting list already living on the Island wanted to be re-housed there – usually because of family connections. But empty properties on the Island were allocated on a Borough-wide basis, to the homeless or to people who were being decanted to make way for redevelopment. This did not stop hundreds of applicants coming forward to press their claims if a council property on the Island became vacant. Young people began putting their names down on the housing list as soon as they turned sixteen.

When redevelopment began there was hope that this would bring more homes within reach of Islanders, but in fact people felt squeezed out. A "realistically priced" second floor one-bedroom flat on Plymouth Wharf was advertised for sale at over £80,000, and a two-bedroom, two-bathroom apartment in London Yard for £115,000. A survey in 1985 showed that 75% of households in the three Docklands Boroughs had annual incomes of below £10,000 and in many cases substantially less.

Concessions which developers made to local people were short lived and reported to be widely abused (for instance through a black market in Council rent books, used to prove local residence). Frustration was partly channelled into "self-build" schemes but these could help only a limited number. Alongside unemployment, the shortage of affordable housing was a burning issue for several years, hotly debated at meetings, discussed in the local press, with outrage expressed in graffiti and sporadic vandalism directed against the "yuppies" in their fortress style apartment blocks.

North Greenwich Bowls Club celebrates its centenary in 2001, Councillors Martin Young, Julia Mainwaring and Mayor Soyful Alom, with club president Albert Hughes.

Summer, 1984, the entrance to Clipper Quay from East Ferry Road / Spindrift Avenue.

A new turn of the screw in the housing shortage came when, in order to make room for the Limehouse Link road, large numbers of people were decanted from an estate in Limehouse into new housing on the Island at Timber Wharves. The fact that many of these incoming Island residents were Bengali only served to make the matter worse in some people's eyes.

Unable to build more homes for rent, the local authority spent money on improving existing stock. In the 1990s it was housing associations, joining forces with the Borough and private investors, who provided new affordable housing on the Island.

By the mid-1990s the Island population was much more varied than it had been twenty years earlier. The working-class population, of mixed ethnic background but predominantly white, was still there. "You can pick out the old Island families even now if you walk round. If you're going past Cubitt Town School – there's still a hard core of old Island-type families, you know, children and grandchildren. You recognise their faces as well. It was a very close community, this was the thing." (Bessie B.1997)

There were newer residents who had found a place in the community through involvement in schools, churches or social life. There were those who lived isolated lives, getting by on the dole or as single parents in lonely flats; those who passing through, waiting for a move off the Island, or spending their student days here.

There were Bengali people, sustained by strong family and cultural networks, but often disadvantaged in other ways. The old community had been isolated and had nourished a traditional anxiety about "strangers". This sentiment turned into outright expressions of racism against Bengali families. They were seen as taking homes which could have been allocated to existing residents, and they were vulnerable in a way which the rich young professional home buyers were not. Notoriously, in 1993 the grievances of the white working-class community were exploited by the British National Party, which succeeding in winning a council seat on the Island and holding it for a few months. Bengali residents suffered persistent racism:

"I live on the Isle of Dogs and I think it is a nice place to live. The main thing that annoys me is when I get leaflets though the door saying support the BNP which I don't like at all. I like the schools because there are all different colours and we can all get on with each other." Vicky, *Stories from the Island*, 1994.

However, Bengali people felt they had a contribution to make: "My grandfather came here to work in the naval ship and fought in the war. My father came here as a semi-skilled labourer and earned money. And then we came here as a settled family with full right of abode, and I became a barrister. How nice the changing steps of our history are!" (Nazir, *Island History essay.*)

Another noticeable addition to the Island population were the young professionals, singles and couples, childless and first-time home-owners in apartments conveniently close to well-paid work in the new financial centre; and older people, high-flyers in publishing or financial services, also living and working locally, sometimes on short-term contracts and often with second homes elsewhere. These two groups included people of all nationalities – global workers in the global markets, and their life-style was noticeably different from that of more established residents

"They're finding jobs for different people over in the Docklands, but these people what's coming over, they reckon some of 'em's very uppish and one thing and the other, so we're the poor relations to them, sort of thing, still it don't bother me, don't bother me." (Lucy Banks)

"...when some of the newcomers come to the Island and try to impress us with their wealth, their expensive homes and cars, their better education, no wonder we turn away or equally brag to regain our pride – we are made to feel that we are worthless and it hurts!" (Joan C.)

"One World Week" 2001, celebrated at St. Edmund's Roman Catholic Church, Westferry Road, with a congregation of 270, in which 41 nations were represented, some of them seen here sampling the food of different cultures.

In the decades of redevelopment, enormous and complicated challenges faced the schools, churches, local clubs, amenity projects, tenants' associations and campaigning groups on the Island. They had been vibrant and active in the 1970s, when the provision of housing and jobs was deteriorating, transport and schooling were poor, and the future uncertain. They had made many gains, largely as a result of grass roots initiatives and the hard work of committed individuals. Many of the community projects and groups of the 1980s and 1990s had their roots in the 1970s, including *The Islander* newspaper, the AIC itself, the tenants' associations, the Mudchute Park and Farm, the Island History Trust, the Dockland Sailing Centre, the Island Advice Centre, the Space, the facilities for pre-school age children, pensioners' clubs

and several community centres.

During the redevelopment, local organisations still had their traditional role of providing a range of support and leisure services; but they were doing this at a time when all the worst aspects of the rebuilding programme were being felt on the Island and when the population was more deeply divided along the lines of race and class than it had ever been before. The needs were greater than ever, for good social amenities for everyone and for projects which would provide meeting places for different sections of the population. But resources were at a low ebb. Council budgets were restricted (there were cuts of up to 44% in 1991) and the Corporation did not see itself as responsible for social regeneration.

Through persistent effort, local pressure groups, of which the Association of Island Communities was one, were able to impress the corporation and the government with the need to address social needs at the same time as promoting economic development. A House of Lords Select Committee on Employment, discussing the issue, concluded that: "It is not good for the health of a community for the original inhabitants of an area to see others benefitting, as they see it, at their expense, while they suffer from increased road traffic congestion, higher house prices and associated ills. Nor is it just."

The arrival on the scene of Canadian developers Olympia and York helped matters – they were experienced in the value of tackling local issues and were said to be appalled at the "social mess" they found.

As a result, from the late 1980s, the Corporation and the new businesses moving into the area, made money available for education, training, leisure and the support of a range of services aimed at addressing social needs. The notion of "planning gain" was adopted, whereby developers contributed to community benefit, in return for planning concessions. At the same time, local opposition gradually gave way to acceptance of the developers and a desire to work with them, rather than against them.

The virulent racism of the early 1990s subsided

Top picture opposite: Islanders on an outing to the docks and shipyards of Holland in 1985, organised by the Island History Trust. Left to right: Eileen and Bernard Bannister, friend, Olive Campbell, Valerie Martin, Phyllis Whalley, Maud Dyer, Arthur Wiggins, Vera (nee Munden), Iris Johnson, Nell Humphries, Lily Bennett, Eve Hostettler, Doris McCartney, Les Towler, Martha McCartney, friend, Betty Coombes, Ada Price, Jasmine and George Pye, Sylvia and Peter Wade, Arthur Coombes, Buddy and John Penn, Tony Wailey, Doris Muldoon. Picture by Mike Seaborne.

Lower picture: The Docklands Armada, waterborne demonstration, early 1980s.

and Bengali people felt it was safer to walk the streets. As one youth worker said: "This is their home". He pointed out the barriers in the way of integration and understanding, but there were meeting places for the different cultures in schools, community centres and sports clubs.

At the end of the century, it could still be said that the Isle of Dogs "was in many ways unique" – but it was not the isolated backwater it had been, nor was it any longer a working-class community centred around industry and the work of the Port. The redevelopment had favoured the rich, and had created new divisions.

The problems of a housing shortage, and unemployment, persisted. Community leaders were aware of a tendency for grass roots initiatives to be hampered by increasing bureaucracy.

The face of the Island was changing in a changing world and no-one could predict what the new millenium might bring. Yet the Island still had a certain magic: "I love it here, the people are friendly, and I don't want to move" said a new resident.

The Island Carnival at the junction of East Ferry Road and Glengall Grove, 1988.

Bill Smith looking through the Photograph Collection at the Island
History Open Days, George Green Centre, December 1984.

Sources

Books

Burnett, John, *A Social History of Housing 1815-1970*, Methuen Press, 1980

Calder, Angus, *The People's War*, Pimlico, 1996

Carr, R.J.M., editor, *Dockland*, North East London Polytechnic/GLC, 1986

Foster, Janet, *Docklands, Cultures in Conflict, Worlds in Collision*, UCL Press, 1999

Palmer, Alan, *The East End, Four Centuries of London Life*, John Murray, 2000

Pudney, John, *London's Docks*, Thames & Hudson, 1975

White, Jerry, *London in the Twentieth Century*, Penguin/Viking. 2001

Other Material

Rising East, The Journal of East London Studies, volume 2, No.2, "LDDC Special Issue", Lawrence & Wishart, 1998

Cole, Thomas J, *Life & Labor in the Isle of Dogs, The Origins and Evolution of an East London Working Class Community, 1800-1980*, Ph.D. Dissertation, unpublished, University of Oklahoma 1984

Collections of transcripts, letters, essays and stories donated by Islanders to the Island History Trust Collection 1980-2001.

Newspapers etc., housed in the Local Studies Archive, Central Library, Bancroft Road, London E1.

Illustrations

The following sources of pictures are gratefully acknowledged:
Museum in Docklands: pages 20, 21, 37, 85, 86 and 87
National Monuments Record: page 77
London Borough of Tower Hamlets: pages 31, 70 and 99
Times Newspapers Limited: inside back cover
Richard H. Smith: page 135
Mike Seaborne took photographs reproduced on the front cover and pages 1, 4, 94, 116, 118, 119, 120, 121, 122, 123, 125, 127, and 130.
Derek Chambers took the photograph on page 2.

Index to Volumes I & II

134

Ada Price, Chairwoman of Island History, with Michael Foot MP, and Eve Hostettler, curator of Island History. The Trust was awarded the Raymond Williams Prize for Community Literature in 1994.